Receiving
the Gifts of the
Holy Spirit

BILL SUBRITZKY

Sovereign World

DEDICATION

To my dear wife Pat,
who has been such a faithful helpmate
over many years.

Sovereign World Ltd
P.O. Box 17
Chichester PO20 6YB
England

International edition 1986

All Scripture quotations are from the New King James Bible.

Copyright © 1979, 1980, 1982 Thomas Nelson Inc.

ISBN 1 85240 000 5

Printed and Bound in Great Britain by
Whitstable Litho Ltd., Whitstable, Kent

CONTENTS

FOREWORD

Bill Subritzky is a layman, in the language of the church. He was senior partner in a large legal firm and founder and governing director of one of the largest homebuilding companies in New Zealand. But he is no ordinary layman. In fact, he ministers in a realm and with a sense of authority totally foreign to many clergymen.

The fact that he has held every position open to a lay member of the Anglican church is not what makes him unusual. Rather, it is his discovery of the New Testament doctrine of the priesthood of believers and the appropriation of this truth to a degree that many have missed.

Bill Subritzky's story is much more than that of a capable churchman transformed into a Spirit-filled servant of God. It is the account of a man in whom the risen Christ dwells and through whom the Holy Spirit imparts spiritual gifts. This book reveals the burden of a man who has a burning desire to share the spiritual discoveries that have revolutionized his life.

The messages in this book were delivered at the 1981 World Convention of Full Gospel Business Men's Fellowship International, Philadelphia, Pennsylvania, USA; the transcription has been edited with every effort to preserve the style and spirit which so profoundly stirred thousands.

God has opened doors for the author to minister in places far from his native New Zealand, including the Philippines, Singapore, Canada and the United States. Wherever he ministers, the experience is as though he were delivering and unwrapping beautiful spiritual gifts from God, to be used and enjoyed by ordinary people.

The Christian community needs this book. Someone has seen the church today as analogous to a football stadium in which overworked pastors are like 22 exhausted players desperately needing rest, viewed by 50,000 spectators badly in need of exercise. *Receiving the Gifts of the Holy Spirit* is a call to all Spirit-filled believers to get out of the bleachers and to assume their responsibilities and privileges as the kings and priests God intended them to be.

NELSON B. MELVIN, D.D.

Senior Editor, Voice Magazine

PREFACE

Since 1971, when I was baptized in the Holy Spirit, I have felt that many people greatly desire to operate fully in the gifts of the Holy Spirit as set forth in I Corinthians 12 (the word of wisdom, the word of knowledge, faith, the gifts of healing, miracles, prophecy, discerning of spirits, tongues and interpretation of tongues).

I fervently believe that God has placed these gifts within the body of Christ for the purpose of edification, especially during these last days. Wherever I find churches operating in these gifts I see there is a refreshing spiritual aliveness within these churches.

Sensing a yearning for this on the part of many believers, in this book I have endeavoured to explain how I began to move in the gifts. Led by the Holy Spirit, I have tried to do this in a very simple way.

I trust that as you read these pages God will richly bless you and give you a deeper understanding of His blessings.

Since the first edition was published in 1981 I have found that the Holy Spirit has led me in further ways in which to encourage christians to move in the gifts of the Holy Spirit.

He has also further clarified for me the nature of some of the gifts. Accordingly I have expanded upon the anointing of God chapter five, and have added a clearer definition of the word of wisdom in chapter seven, of the word of knowledge chapter eight, of prophecy in chapter twelve, and of interpretation of tongues in chapter fifteen. In addition I have added a new chapter seventeen called "Learning in Groups".

I am very hopeful that with these
additions this edition
will prove even more helpful
than the earlier editions.

ONE

Belief Required

The great outpouring of God's Spirit around the world, particularly during the decade of the '60s and '70s, in what is commonly called the charismatic renewal, has created a definite resurgence of interest in the gifts of the Holy Spirit. Described in I Corinthians 12:8-10, they are the gifts of the word of wisdom, the word of knowledge, faith, healing, miracles, prophecy, discerning of spirits, kinds of tongues and interpretations of tongues.

I believe that the gifts of the Holy Spirit are available to and are to be exercised by all members of the body of Christ who are prepared to reach out to God and believe for them. I have been privileged on numerous occasions to stand before a congregation and pray for the sick by the word of knowledge, or to pray for deliverance and cast out demons, or to operate in various areas of faith, and I have sensed in my spirit a deep yearning on the part of many people to be involved in this area of ministry. Over the years the Lord has told me that whatever I have learned I should share with others, encouraging them to enter into these gifts.

After twenty years of church attendance, I came to know Jesus Christ as my personal Saviour. At that point in time, I was also baptized in the Holy Spirit. The experience transformed my total thinking as a lawyer and businessman. Once I opened the Word of God and began to understand it for the first time in my life, I became so hungry for it that I wanted to move quickly into the gifts of the Holy Spirit.

The starting point, I believe, and a first essential for moving in the gifts, is of course to be born again and to be baptized in the Holy Spirit.

I always tell people that if they wish the gifts of 1 Corinthians 12, they should be prepared to go the full extent of receiving the experience of the baptism in the Holy Spirit, enabling them to move in God's full power.

In Luke's gospel we find the risen Jesus telling His disciples:

> *And, behold, I send the promise of my Father upon you: but tarry ye in the city of Jerusalem, until ye be endued with power from on high* (Luke 24:49).

Again, in Acts we find these words which He spoke to the disciples after His resurrection:

> *But ye shall receive power, after that the Holy Ghost is come upon you: and ye shall be witnesses unto me both in Jerusalem, and in all Judea, and in Samaria, and unto the uttermost part of the earth* (Acts 1:8).

As we know, this power came upon them on the day of Pentecost. We find it described in the Book of Acts:

> *And when the day of Pentecost was fully come, they were all with one accord in one place.*
>
> *And suddenly there came a sound from heaven as of a rushing mighty wind, and it filled all the house where they were sitting.*
>
> *And there appeared unto them cloven tongues like as of fire, and it sat upon each of them.*
>
> *And they were all filled with the Holy Ghost, and began to speak with other tongues, as the Spirit gave them utterance* (Acts 2:1-4).

Anyone who has given his life to Jesus Christ and who acknowledges Him as Lord and Saviour can easily come into this experience if he seeks it with all his heart.

I have been privileged to pray for many thousands of people to be baptized in the Holy Spirit. It is my experience that if people are properly taught and their hearts are really open to the Lord, then only a small percentage fail to come immediately into the gift of tongues. Putting all fear and prejudice aside, we need to become as little children. Jesus affirms:

> *... Except ye be converted, and become as little children, ye shall not enter into the kingdom of heaven* (Matthew 18:3).

To those desirous of receiving the baptism in the Holy Spirit and speaking in tongues, I have found it helpful to cite examples of how as little children they made sounds their parents taught them in their native language, whether it were English or any other language. I usually encourage people to say the word A*bba*, which is the very personal Hebrew word for F*ather*. This is a good word to start with because it is a word of adoration for God and also because it is unfamiliar to their ears. Having prayed for Jesus the Baptizer to baptize them in the Holy Ghost, I then encourage them to start with the word A*bba*. Syllables begin to come from their mouths, and as they are further encouraged a language flows forth.

We are all different in the way we react, but we all need encouragement and love to come into these experiences. God himself plants the seed of faith in our hearts. However, He asks us to exercise it. As we do so, He is able to bless.

A total and complete belief in the Word of God is essential. This was difficult for me as a lawyer, before I was saved and baptized in the Holy Ghost. When I was attending church without a Christ-centered commitment, I had a belief in the Word of God that was intellectual and not from my heart. One of the wonderful things that happened to me when I was baptized in the Holy Spirit was that belief in the Word of God was transferred from my mind to my heart. This totally transformed my understanding of the Word. I then had absolute belief in the Word of God.

What actually brought me to the point of faith? It was a complete and childlike acceptance of the Bible as the Word of God. I was convinced in myself, without any question, without any doubts, without any fear, that *this is the Word of God!*

The significance of this firm faith in God's Word was strongly brought to my attention not long after I began to operate in the gifts. When I began to quote scriptures to people with demonic problems, the demons would begin to scream out of them. When the demons know that you mean and believe what you say (and I believe in some circumstances demons can sense your feelings and thoughts), they will move, but not before. When I speak the Word of God with total belief, then the demons begin to scream, particularly if I quote such verses as —

. . . death and hell were cast into the lake of fire (Rev. 20:14)

I also tell the demons that their final destination will be the lake of fire. They begin to scream. "No, no, *no*, we don't want to hear those words!"

Total belief in the authenticity of the Word of God is essential in the operation of any gift of the Spirit. When you are walking close to the Lord and you believe you are getting something from God, then He gives you that additional faith to move ahead. You cannot, for example, operate in the gift of healing without a full certainty that by the stripes of Jesus we were healed. People endeavour to operate at a shallow level in the gifts and therefore never get very far with it.

Not too long after I came into the baptism in the Spirit I was confronted with an emergency situation while driving in my car. I realized I was out of fuel. The logical thing was for me to stop the car and try to obtain some. But in this new experience of the baptism in the Holy Spirit, and with a sudden faith in the Word of God, believing at that moment that this was the will of God for me, I prayed that my tank would be filled.

Although I had travelled many miles up hill and down, the gas indicator had remained firmly pointed to the "empty" position during the last few miles. There was no mistake about the position of the needle. As I prayed, to my utter astonishment the needle began to rise! Now, that astonished my natural mind, but not my spirit. The Lord provided sufficient gasoline for me to complete the emergency job I had to accomplish at that time. Beyond that, He enabled me to travel a considerable distance until I finally realized it was time I went off the Lord's fuel supply and back to filling up my car tank on regular gasoline.

That experience gave me a quality of faith in the Word of God which has never left me. Inside the front cover of my Bible I have inscribed these words which describe both my understanding of and belief in God's Word:

This is the Word of God.
It is supernatural in origin,
eternal in duration,
inexpressible in value,
infinite in scope,
regenerative in power,
infallible in authority,
universal in interest,
personal in application,
inspired in totality.
Read it through,
write it down,
pray it in,
work it out,
then pass it on.

And that has been my testimony for the last fourteen years as I have believed implicitly in His Word.

TWO

Distinguishing Between Gifts and Fruit of the Spirit

It is important to distinguish between the gifts of the Holy Spirit as set out in I Corinthians 12:8-10, and the fruit of the Holy Spirit referred to in Galatians 5:22-23. In the Galatians passage we find that the fruit of the Spirit is love, joy, peace, long-suffering, gentleness, goodness, faith, meekness, and temperance.

I was rather stunned in the early years of my Christian walk when I found men moving in great gifts of the Holy Spirit who considered themselves to be remarkable, anointed men of God, but whose personal lives left much to be desired. As I came close to those men, such experiences almost shattered me as a young Christian. I recognized that there was great sin in their lives. Then as I searched in the Scriptures I began to realize that the gifts of God are in fact given without repentance. Concerning this, the Book of Romans declares,

> ... *the gifts and calling of God are without repentance* (Romans 11:29).

Thus, when God gives something He gives it fully and does not recall it. We ourselves can abandon it or stray from God, not properly functioning in the gifts and thereby losing the power of the Holy Spirit.

I also began to better comprehend the meaning of what Jesus said in the Gospel of Matthew:

> *Every tree that bringeth not forth good fruit is hewn down, and cast into the fire.*
>
> *Wherefore by their fruits ye shall know them.*
>
> *Not every one that saith unto me, Lord, Lord, shall enter into the kingdom of heaven; but he that doeth the will of my Father which is in heaven.*
>
> *Many will say to me in that day, Lord, Lord, have we not prophesied in thy name? and in thy name have cast out devils? and in thy name done many wonderful works?*
>
> *And then will I profess unto them, I never knew you: depart from me, ye that work iniquity* (Matthew 7:19-23).

Thus, only those who have done the will of the Father will enter the kingdom, even though such persons may have prophesied and cast out devils. Therefore, if we are to enter the kingdom of God we must be obedient to the Word of God and follow His commandments. Above all, we must obey the new commandment of loving one another as He loved us.

God does not wait until we are perfect before He gives us gifts. He offers us the gifts of the Holy Spirit when we turn to Him in faith and believe His Word. The first gift referred to in the New Testament is the gift of righteousness. God offers this to us even while we are in sin. It is Christ's righteousness that we received as part of our salvation, when we turn to Him in true repentance.

He does not wait until we are holy and perfect before He offers us this gift.

Likewise, He does not wait until we are perfect before offering us the gifts of the Holy Spirit. Jesus said in Matthew's gospel,

> *Ask, and it shall be given you; seek, and ye shall find; knock, and it shall be opened unto you:*
>
> *For every one that asketh receiveth; and he that seeketh findeth; and to him that knocketh it shall be opened.*
>
> *Or what man is there of you, whom if his son ask bread, will he give him a stone?*
>
> *Or if he ask a fish, will he give him a serpent?*
>
> *If ye then, being evil, know how to give good gifts unto your children, how much more shall your Father which is in heaven give good things to them that ask him?* (Matthew 7:7-11).

It is very important for us to understand the difference between the gifts of the Spirit and the fruit of the Spirit. We read in Galatians:

> *And they that are Christ's have crucified the flesh with the affections and lusts* (Galatians 5:24).

The fruit of the Spirit belongs to the Spirit, and as we walk close to the Lord these are evidenced in our lives. They — not the gifts of the Spirit — will be the basis for our judgment by the Lord.

Incidentally, I have noticed one interesting point in connection with spiritual purity. The gift of discernment, extremely beneficial in casting out devils, requires that one's life be reasonably clean. If sin reigns in some area of your life and you begin to cast a devil out of another person, Satan will repeatedly accuse you, and you will become an ineffective instrument. One reason, I believe, that these particular gifts are not greatly exercised is that the "accuser of the brethren" begins to express his true nature. If there is sin in your life and you are trying to cast out a demon based on sin in another person's life, you will find that sooner or later you will begin to lose certainty in what you are trying to do.

Having sounded that word of caution, it is important that we should keep a balance. Some people have majored in the fruit of the Spirit; some have specialized in the gifts of the Spirit; but I believe we should be aware of the spiritual balance. God wants the gifts of the Spirit to flow in the body of Christ in order to edify, exhort, comfort, and build us up. That is why the gifts of the Spirit should be exercised in our churches, along with the fruit of the Spirit blossoming in our lives.

A real surge of spiritual life begins to manifest itself in a fresh way in the local church as encouragement is given through the exercise of the gifts.

THREE

Finding Our Place in the Body of Christ

The next requirement for moving in the gifts is to find our place in the body of Christ. This is defined very clearly in Romans 12:1-6 in a clear statement of certain principles. Paul says,

I beseech you therefore, brethren, by the mercies of God, that ye present your bodies a living sacrifice, holy, acceptable unto God, which is your reasonable service (Romans 12:1).

So the first step, if we are going to move in the gifts of God, including the other gifts in 1 Corinthians 12, is to present our bodies a living sacrifice. We must yield our bodies as well as our minds to God. It is a yielding of ourselves to Him. We find the second step in the next verse:

And be not conformed to this world; but be ye transformed by the renewing of your mind . . . (Romans 12:2).

If we come to Jesus Christ as a little child and receive Him as Saviour, we begin to receive a spiritual mind.

For to be carnally minded is death; but to be spiritually minded is life and peace.

> *Because the carnal mind is enmity against God: for it is not subject to the law of God, neither indeed can be* (Romans 8:6,7).

Our natural mind will never understand the things of God. Paul vividly explains this:

> *But the natural man receiveth not the things of the Spirit of God: for they are foolishness unto him: neither can he know them, because they are spiritually discerned* (I Corinthians 2:14).

While I was a church attender but not a committed Christian, I was chairman of a group of representatives drawn from a number of Christian congregations. We met together frequently in my home, and I was always impressed by the quiet demeanour of one man. He said very little, but when he did speak, it was well worth giving our attention. I sensed in him a deep understanding of the Word of God.

One night after one of the meetings he said, "Bill, you will never understand the Bible until you are really born again. The things of God are spiritually discerned, and until you are born again you lack insight into biblical truth."

I protested vigorously that I could read the Bible as well as he could, but I knew deep in my heart that this was not true. Many times I would open the Bible but I failed to understand what it meant. It was only when I became as a little child, humbled myself before God, asked Him to forgive me of my sins and invited Jesus to be Lord of my life, that suddenly I was transformed in my mind and the Word of God opened up to me.

Having been transformed in our mind, we find the following:

> *. . . that ye may prove what is that good, and acceptable, and perfect will of God* (Romans 12:2)

This is the next step. Notice that it is in an ascending order, beginning first at good, going on to acceptable, and finally to perfect.

I found that in order to begin to move in the gifts of God I had to have my mind transformed, so I might find what is the good, then the acceptable, then the perfect, will of God. This came as the result of obedience to the Word of God.

God has given each of us a measure of faith.

> For I say, through the grace given unto me, to every man that is among you, not to think of himself more highly than he ought to think; but to think soberly, according as God hath dealt to every man the measure of faith (Romans 12:3).

Every one has a measure of faith which God has given. As we begin to find our place in the body of Christ that faith increases.

Paul says,

> For as we have many members in one body, and all members have not the same office:
> So we, being many, are one body in Christ, and every one members one of another (Romans 12:4,5).

It is imperative for us to find our place in the body of Christ. We cannot be loners; we must be a member of some part of the body of Christ. Attendance at a local church where Jesus Christ is Lord and where He is worshipped as such is an essential ingredient in moving in the gifts of God. If we are prepared to find our place in a local body of believers in Christ, submitting to the authority structure of that group, then God is able to bless us abundantly. We need to be encouraged by one another; hence, the need to be members of a part of the body of Christ where we can receive that encouragement. When I began to move in the gifts of the Spirit, I was encouraged by a local body of believers who shared with me and said, "We want to encourage you into these gifts." It was in that way that I began to move in the gifts of the Holy Spirit.

One of the weapons Satan uses against the children of God is pride. Once we begin to move in the gifts of God, temptation enters our minds in an attempt to deceive us into thinking that we are in some measure better than the next person. In this way, Satan attacks us and our ministry, our natural mind comes into play, and we may begin to hear from ourselves rather than from God. It is necessary for that part of the body of Christ of which we are members to be able to discern that we are really operating in the gifts of God under the anointing of the Holy Spirit and not under some other spirit.

This is why Jesus said,

> *And whosoever shall exalt himself shall be abased; and he that shall humble himself shall be exalted* (Matthew 23:12).

We must humble ourselves before the body of Christ as we use the gifts so that there may be real discernment and love in testing those gifts. If we are not prepared to submit to the authority in a local part of the body, we are in very real danger of possible misuse of the gifts and spiritual fruitlessness.

Now we come to the last step:

> *Having then gifts differing according to the grace that is given to us, whether prophecy, let us prophesy according to the proportion of faith;*
>
> *Or ministry, let us wait on our ministering; or he that teacheth, on teaching;*

Or he that exhorteth, on exhortation: he that giveth, let him do it with simplicity; he that ruleth, with diligence; he that sheweth mercy, with cheerfulness (Romans 12:6,7,8).

It is only then that we have the gifts.

So possessing spiritual gifts and properly exercising them is the culmination of adhering to God's established pattern for your life.

FOUR

Receiving the Gifts of the Holy Spirit

There has been an emphasis in the previous chapter on the need to be part of the body of Christ. As part of the body we can receive the gifts of the Holy Spirit in a scriptural way by the laying on of hands.

Paul says, in the Epistle to the Romans,

For I long to see you, that I may impart unto you some spiritual gift, to the end ye may be established;

That is, that I may be comforted together with you by the mutual faith both of you and me (Romans 1:11,12).

Here Paul is clearly showing a desire to impart gifts to others and a belief that he can do so under the anointing of the Spirit of God. Thus, it is no surprise to read in his letter to the young disciple Timothy,

Wherefore I put thee in remembrance that thou stir up the gift of God, which is in thee by the putting on of my hands (II Timothy 1:6).

It is clear that Paul laid hands on Timothy to receive the gifts of the Holy Spirit.

Again, we find him saying,

> *Neglect not the gift that is in thee, which was given thee by prophecy, with the laying on of the hands of the presbytery* (I Timothy 4:14).

It is obvious that the elders gathered together for the laying on of hands, including Paul's, and that prophecy was given at this time.

Paul also says,

> *This charge I commit unto thee, son Timothy, according to the prophecies which went before on thee, that thou by them mightest war a good warfare* (I Timothy 1:18).

I have found that this is an excellent way in which to encourage people to receive the gifts of the Holy Spirit.

For a number of years I have gone to a certain church and prayed with the elders for the impartation of the gifts of the Spirit upon them. At first I prayed with the elders, laying hands on each of them. I find that if I wait upon the Lord, He begins to quicken to me the various gifts which He desires to impart to a person at that time, and by faith I speak them out. My wife Pat, who operates in the gift of prophecy, then brings a prophecy for that person which further builds them up. It is a privilege to return to that church each year and to see these gifts being more deeply ministered, as the elders themselves lay hands on other members of the congregation.

Some years ago, teaching along these lines at a conference in Melbourne, Australia, I invited a number of the clergy to come forward. After I prayed for the first person, laid hands upon him, and spoke out those gifts which I believed the Holy Spirit was bringing to mind, Pat gave a prophecy; I immediately encouraged that person to lay hands on the next in line. As he did so the Lord began to bring to his mind the gifts which the Lord desired to impart upon that person. As these were spoken out I myself witnessed to each one of them. Then each of those two people laid hands on the next person, and again the same procedure occurred — and so on, until we had prayed for all the clergy. Before we had gone very far down the line the power of God had fallen upon us and a number of the clergy were slain in the Spirit as the power of God touched them.

When I pray I usually use such words as, "I ask You, Lord Jesus, to impart these and such other gifts as You would upon our brother (or sister)." We cannot limit God, and it may well be that there are gifts for that person to receive other than those which are quickened to us at that moment.

As hands have been laid on persons to receive gifts in this way, I have seen mighty things happen: people healed at that moment; people receiving a public tongue; interpretation and prophesying. I would therefore encourage you to remember this scriptural basis for receiving the gifts; namely, by the laying on of hands.

I do not believe God is limited to that method, but it is wonderful, if you are moving in the love of the body of Christ in your church, to ask the elders to lay hands upon you for the gifts of the Spirit. This is very important, since it is in the body of Christ that the gifts begin to be discerned. People begin to say, "I believe, brother (or sister) you have the gift of prophecy" (or it may be the discernment of spirits, or the gift of faith, or the gift of healing). You become encouraged in the body of Christ by those who love you in Jesus.

Most of what I have learned concerning the gifts of the Spirit has been at small prayer meetings where the love of Jesus was present. It was then that I began to hear His voice, of which I will have more to say later.

FIVE

The Anointing of God

Before we look finally at the gifts referred to in I Corinthians 12, I would refer to the anointing of God:

> But the anointing which ye have received of him abideth in you, and ye need not that any man teach you: but as the same anointing teacheth you of all things, and is truth, and is no lie, and even as it hath taught you, ye shall abide in him (I John 2:27).

The anointing is also referred to in I John 2:20.

> But you have an anointing from the Holy One and you know all things.

Put it another way

> But ye have an unction from the Holy One and ye know all things.

It is clear therefore that we have within us an anointing. How does this come into us?

The anointing is part of the operation of the Holy Spirit within us, Jesus said in John 16:13:

> Howbeit when he, the Spirit of truth, is come, he will guide you into all truth: for he shall not speak of himself; but whatsoever he shall hear, that shall he speak: and he will show you things to come.

The Holy Spirit has come into the world to speak to us the things which He hears from God.

In the Old Testament we have a clear indication that an anointing oil consisting of myrrh, sweet cinnamon, calamus, cassia and olive oil was used to anoint kings and prophets. This is set out in Exodus 30:23-30.

> Take thou also unto thee principal spices, of pure myrrh five hundred shekels, and of sweet cinnamon half so much, even two hundred and fifty shekels, and of sweet calamus two hundred and fifty shekels,
>
> And of cassia five hundred shekels, after the shekel of the sanctuary, and of oil olive an hin:
>
> And thou shalt make it an oil of holy ointment, an ointment compound after the art of the apothecary: it shall be an holy anointing oil.
>
> And thou shalt anoint the tabernacle of the congregation therewith, and the ark of the testimony,
>
> And the table and all his vessels, and the candlestick and his vessels, and the alter of incense,
>
> And the altar of burnt offering with all his vessels, and the laver and his foot.
>
> And thou shalt sanctify them, that they may be most holy: whatsoever toucheth them shall be holy.
>
> And thou shalt anoint Aaron and his sons, and consecrate them, that they may minister unto me in the priest's office.

We find that Moses subsequently poured the anointing oil on Aaron's head as he was instructed in order to anoint him and sanctify him, i.e. set him apart. Thus we find in Leviticus the following quotation:

> *And he poured of the anointing oil upon Aaron's head, and anointed him, to sanctify him.* (*Leviticus* 8:12)

Thus it is clear from the Old Testament that the anointing oil consisting of the ingredients set out above was made up and poured on the head of the prophet or priest. It was also poured on the kings when they were anointed and appointed as kings. We find this in the case of both King David and King Saul.

Thus we find the psalmist expressing this experience in the following psalm:

> *It is like the precious ointment upon the head, that ran down upon the beard, even Aaron's beard: that went down to the skirts of his garments;*
> *As the dew of Hermon, and as the dew that descended upon the mountains of Zion: for there the Lord commanded the blessing, even life for ever more.* (*Psalm* 133:2,3).

In that psalm we have a clear picture of the anointing oil being poured on Aaron's head and spreading down through his beard. It is easy to visualise this oil as a warm oil being poured down over Aaron's head so that he had a physical feeling of the oil as it spread over his body.

The oil had a clear fragrance arising from the ingredients and this fragrance was expressed as being on the garments of Jesus who is our High Priest.

> *All thy garments smell of myrrh, and aloes, and cassia, out of the ivory palaces, whereby they have made thee glad.* (*Psalm* 45:8).

I find that in many meetings where there is a real anointing of the Holy Spirit, one can smell the fragrance of the Holy Spirit. It is a clearly distinguishable and beautiful perfume, quite the opposite of the horrible smell that is associated with Satan and his demons. Many people are able to physically smell the presence of the Lord as they smell this perfume at the meetings. At the same time many are immediately healed as the anointing falls upon them.

Turning to the New Testament we find that believers are kings and priests. For example:

> *But ye are a chosen generation, a royal priesthood, an holy nation, a peculiar people; that ye should shew forth the praises of him who hath called you out of darkness into his marvellous light:* (I Peter 2:9).

Thus we see we are a royal priesthood. Again we find further reference in the Book of Revelation:

> *And hath made us kings and priests unto God and his Father; to him be glory and dominion for ever and ever. Amen. (Revelation 1:6).*

Thus the believer is described as being a king and priest and as such God would want to anoint the believer and set him aside for God's glory.

We find confirmation of this in Paul's letter to the Corinthians.

> *Now he which establisheth us with you in Christ, and hath anointed us, is God. (2 Cor 1:21).*

When I first came into the things of the Holy Spirit, I initiated a prayer meeting in our home. As the weeks went by and the meetings continued week after week, brethren from other churches (including the Pentecostal churches) came along to help us in operating the gifts of the Spirit.

I am Anglican by denomination. A large percentage of the population in New Zealand claim adherence to that church group. I am always grateful for the man who came for thirty-six meetings (that is, one each week for a period of nine months). He would stand with me as I prayed for other people because I was believing in the Word of God for healing. He went around the meeting praying for the sick.

As I was praying he would ask, "Brother Bill, do you sense the anointing of the Holy Spirit?" I would say, "I don't sense a thing." He would say, "Well, the Holy Spirit is here, I sense His presence." Every week this would take place — but I did not sense the presence of the Holy Spirit. However, when God puts the spirit of faith into your heart you hang in there, and for those thirty-six meetings I persevered, believing for the anointing of God.

Then one night we were standing with an elderly lady, and this brother asked, "Do you sense the anointing of the Holy Spirit?" At that very moment I felt the heavens open and I sensed the anointing, that beautiful warmth like soothing oil from God, falling upon me. I have known this anointing ever since as I have turned my face, my faith, and my heart towards Jesus in every circumstance, putting my natural mind aside. It had been my *mind* — even though I was baptized in the Holy Spirit — which had blocked me from knowing that anointing of God.

We do not always come immediately into the anointing of the Holy Spirit. In Singapore some years ago at the invitation of the Anglican Bishop Chiu, a man of God who has moved in things of the Spirit for a number of years, we were together at the Singapore Cathedral when he expressed interest in the experience of the anointing of the Holy Spirit. As I will explain in Chapter 12, this man came into the anointing simply by a demonstration of the Spirit of God releasing him in that circumstance, and ever since he has moved mightily under that anointing.

You may be saying as you read this, "I would love to know the anointing of God." Let me explain two ways in which I have seen it happen to others. Unbelief or wrong theology can block God's power. On one occasion I was ministering with a well-known churchman when he remarked that he had never sensed the anointing of God. I suggested that he might have a mind block, which can arise as a result of training which questions the credibility of the Bible.

A very humble man, he readily agreed to my suggestion that he renounce this spirit of blockage of mind. As he did so in the name of Jesus, the anointing of God came upon him and he gently fell to the floor, slain under the power of the Holy Spirit. He has known the reality of the anointing ever since then.

A spirit of unbelief can attach itself to our lives as a result of past experiences, even though we have turned our hearts to Jesus Christ. We may need to turn away from something inherited. In New Zealand we have a lodge called the Masons. I find that if a person's father has belonged to that lodge, or if he himself is a member, he is in spiritual bondage. The lodge worships the spirit of Baal and the spirit of Ashtaroth, both of which are forbidden in the Scriptures. Unless one renounces those links, very frequently there is a spiritual blindness which prevents understanding and moving in the Word of God. In this context, with the person's approval, and after his due repentance, I have often commanded that the spirit of unbelief depart from him — and we have seen wonderful things happen.

As I was participating in a seminar in the Fiji Islands with a professor from a theological college, this dear man, filled with the Holy Spirit and speaking in tongues, said to me, "Bill, I have never known the anointing of the Spirit of God. I really cannot understand how people get slain in the Spirit." So at one point when I was praying for a person and sensed there was a strong anointing presence, I called to this professor and asked, "Brother, can't you sense the anointing? It is tremendous at this moment."

He replied, "I don't sense a thing."

I said, "Brother, you *must* sense this anointing. Just renounce all unbelief."

He said, "In the name of Jesus, I renounce unbelief!"

Then I went on to say, "Surely, brother, you feel this anointing!" There was no response. I repeated it — still no response.

I looked over and there he was, flat on his back, resting in the Spirit.

A little while later I saw him with a very large Fijian lady, praying, as was his custom, very quietly. But now, having been loosed from the area of unbelief, he was free, and as the Spirit of God moved through him I saw the inevitable begin to happen. The large Fijian lady began to sway. This brother's head was lowered as he continued his earnest prayer, and before I could reach the lady, she crashed like a giant tree to the floor (fortunately, it was a wooden floor). From then on I saw many people slain in the Spirit under that man's ministry.

If you have not known the anointing of God, I'm not saying you're possessed of demons. Please don't hear me saying that! I am saying that there can be something attached to our minds as a result of our upbringing and circumstances before we come to Jesus that blocks our belief. If we simply repent of it and say, "Jesus, I turn from any unbelief that is in me. Help me, Lord," then as we yield ourselves to Him the anointing of God will begin to flow and we will sense His presence.

We need to know this if we are to pray with faith for others.

SIX

Love

And now abideth faith, hope, charity, these three; but the greatest of these is charity (I Corinthians 13:13).

Before we examine the gifts of the Holy Spirit in detail, it is important that we spend a little time on the question of love. The love we are talking about is the *agape* love shown to us in I Corinthians 13 which comes from God himself and which we may experience only as we move in obedience to Him.

I am always intrigued by the way in which the Holy Spirit led Paul to describe the gifts of the Spirit in I Corinthians 12. In Chapter 13 we find Paul speaking under the anointing of the Holy Spirit about love, before he speaks in Chapter 14 of the exercise of the gifts in the church.

In this way he makes love central to the exercise of the gifts.

I find that the first requirement when I pray for the sick is to show love. For there may be faith, there may be hope; but if there is no love, God is not really able to minister in His fullness through me to the person for whom I am praying. I must remember that I am a member of the body of Christ and that I must treat every other member on the same basis; namely, of laying down my life for that other member.

As people sense that I am endeavouring to show agape love through Jesus, then the compassion of God begins to flow in that situation. They do not feel that they are being judged, and the Spirit of God is able to come in and heal in a dramatic way.

During the last few years God has given me the ability to tell people I love them in Jesus Christ. As I begin to speak out these words with my mouth and hear them with my ears, it does something for me. I find that it releases in those listening a sense of God's presence, power, and anointing.

Everything else is going to fail — but love will remain. Of faith, hope and love, the greatest is love.

I remember attending a Full Gospel Business Men's Fellowship meeting a few years ago when Johnnie Johnson, a black American and assistant secretary to the United States Navy, spoke about love. He spoke of it in a way I had never heard before. He simply oozed God's love!

I observed that after the meeting he did not walk out. He stayed there and practiced what he preached, still praying for the sick into the early hours of the morning. This man taught me an immense amount about the need to express love. As we do, God's Holy Spirit is able to move through us.

When we come together to worship Jesus Christ each of us must be open to let His love flow through us. We must be able to express it to each other, and particularly to the person to whom we are ministering. Often folk tell me that when they come to one of our meetings and sense the Spirit of God's love, pain leaves their bodies.

I believe that all demon power becomes subject to the power of God through His love, and as love is manifested at a public meeting healings begin to take place and people are delivered. I remember a man telling how, when he entered our home where a prayer meeting was in progress, he immediately sensed love. Till that time he had not been a believer, but he walked out of our house a true believer, having given his heart to Jesus Christ.

Do not be afraid to express the love of Jesus Christ to others. Recently I went to tell my archbishop that I loved him in Jesus Christ, and that I wanted his support in the ministry which God had given me. He responded immediately, offering that support.

We all yearn for love. Let us express it and be free. The gifts of the Holy Spirit are wonderful — they are there to build up the body of Christ — and the fruit of the Spirit is even better. But remember that the greatest of all is God's love, manifested through each one of us.

SEVEN

The Word of Wisdom

For to one is given by the Spirit the word of wisdom (I Corinthians 12:8).

I believe that the word of wisdom is an impression or a thought or a vision or the direct audible voice of the Holy Spirit from God about HOW to deal with a situation.

The first gift referred to in the New Testament is the word of wisdom. I believe it is there in first place for a very good reason. As you move in the gifts of the Holy Spirit you must move in God's wisdom.

In Proverbs we find that Christ and wisdom are one and the same:

Wisdom crieth without; she uttereth her voice in the streets:
She crieth in the chief place of concourse, in the openings of the gates: in the city she uttereth her words, saying, How long, ye simple ones, will ye love simplicity? and the scorners delight in their scorning, and fools hate knowledge?
Turn you at my reproof: behold, I will pour out my spirit unto you, I will make known my words unto you (Proverbs 1:20-23).

Again, in I Corinthians we encounter these words:

. . . *Christ the power of God, and the wisdom of God* (I Corinthians 1:24).

But *of him are ye in Christ Jesus, who of God is made unto us wisdom, and righteousness, and sanctification, and redemption* (I Corinthians 1:30).

We must move in Christ and in His wisdom as we move in the gifts of the Spirit. For example, as we begin to move in the gift of the word of knowledge, the Holy Spirit often will reveal to us something concerning a person. Do we blurt it out, or do we wait until the Spirit gives us a freedom to speak of it?

If I have a word of knowledge concerning a person, that he is fornicating, I would not, unless God specifically ordered it, stand up and publicly say, "Brother, you are fornicating." There would be no love in that approach. I would destroy what the Spirit of God was showing me and trying to accomplish in that person's life.

The same applies to the use of other gifts. Though you may be full of a prophecy coming to your lips, the question of *when* you bring it is a crucial issue. If a person were to stand up while I was speaking from the Word and begin to prophesy, I would say, "I am sorry, but you are out of order. I am speaking from the Word of God and you have interrupted me." I do not believe that the Holy Spirit interrupts Himself.

You may not agree with what I am saying, but these are my discoveries. The gift of wisdom is a gift we should all seek ardently, and God offers it very specifically and clearly. He *offers* you a word of wisdom. Sometimes as you wait upon God or minister to a person or pray for him, something may be impressed upon your mind as to how to deal with that situation. If you are working in God, you may be sure that a good word, in the sense of righteousness, propriety and otherwise, is from the Lord. We must guard against operating in that word of wisdom without really grasping that it is of God.

So the word of wisdom is the gift of having a word at the right time concerning a situation. In counselling situations this gift is tremendously useful. Jesus is wisdom, and we must seek to operate in His wisdom and love.

The word of wisdom may come clearly and simply at any moment, as we are filled with the Holy Spirit. Sometimes the Holy Spirit will show you a person is suffering from a very distressful or negative condition. But the fact He has shown you this condition does not mean that you should speak it to that person at that time. That is why I emphasize the need for love. God will open the door to minister at the right time, showing you how to deal with a situation as you move in His love.

There are various ways of expressing a situation like that described. You may say, "I believe you need prayer. Do you need prayer for healing?" Perhaps the person comments that he has a problem, but the Lord is showing you that it is a very much worse problem than the person realizes. You need wisdom in this situation. The Holy Spirit may well quicken to you that a person in a certain part of a meeting has cancer. If I felt compelled by the Holy Spirit to announce this, in order not to introduce fear I would say, "I believe a person who knows they have this condition is present." Otherwise, every person in that part of the meeting might begin to feel he or she had cancer.

When you begin to move in the gifts of the Spirit, Satan

comes along and tries to put fear into people. But if you move in God's love, reassuring people in that situation, the power of God is able to operate fully and the Holy Spirit is not quenched. I have observed that God will usually bring attention to conditions that are well known to the individuals concerned, thus increasing the faith in that meeting. At other times and in other circumstances — as wisdom leads you — when the person is willing to do so, you may freely go through all of the problems in which he is involved.

Wisdom, the first of the gifts named, is, I believe, closely associated with God's love. I find it works this way: as we move in wisdom, and wait on a word of wisdom, God will drop something into our mind which is the right thing to say at that time to a person. But I can only do this when I am moving in the love of God.

So, when people come for counsel, the Holy Spirit will reveal a situation; then God's wisdom often gives me just a simple word of wisdom for that circumstance; and this saves hours of counselling.

Sometimes we give a word from the Lord without realizing we are doing so, but other members of the body of Christ will discern that we are operating in the gift of wisdom.

There is a wonderful word of wisdom which I often receive from the Lord — the word *repentance*. So often folk come to you for counselling and help who have never really repented, deep down in their hearts, of their involvement with the world. They have never repented of sin, and often the Lord will show you that this is the case. Here God's wisdom is a simple word of love, showing them that they really need to surrender totally to the

Holy Spirit if they are to receive what God has for them. That can be a word of God's wisdom.

In other circumstances, the Holy Spirit quickens (makes alive) to you a portion of the Word of God for a person, or in respect to a situation. If you are saturated with the Word of God, reading it on a regular basis, it is readily brought to your mind. With God nothing is impossible; He *can* bring to your mind a word which you cannot recall having read in the Bible, but which you find to be there. However, I believe He expects us to be diligent in His Word.

·So the word of wisdom is a supernatural gift: a word from the Lord for a particular circumstance or situation in which God gives you wisdom from His Word for dealing appropriately with it.

A beautiful example of the way in which Jesus exercised the word of wisdom is found in the Gospel of John. The scribes and Pharisees, having brought to Jesus a woman taken in the very act of adultery, tested Him by reminding Him that the law of Moses commanded that she should be stoned. They asked Him what they should do.

Here are the words Jesus wrote upon the ground.

> He that is without sin among you, let him first cast a stone at her (John 8:7).

In I Kings 16:28, we find God's wonderful gift of wisdom given to Solomon when the two women came to him, claiming the same child. Solomon commands that a sword be brought to him, then gives instructions that the living child is to be cut in two — one half, to one woman; the other half, to the other. The true mother of the child is easily identified, for immediately she wants the child to be given to the other woman in order to save its life, whereas the other woman would have the child divided.

The apostle James says, concerning wisdom:

> *If any of you lack wisdom, let him ask of God, that giveth to all men liberally, and upbraideth not; and it shall be given him.*
>
> *But let him ask in faith, nothing wavering. For he that wavereth is like a wave of the sea driven with the wind and tossed.*
>
> *For let not that man think that he shall receive any thing of the Lord* (James 1:5,6,7).

Perhaps the simplest way to describe the word of wisdom is that it is a thought, an impression, a vision or the direct audible voice of the Holy Spirit telling us how to deal with the situation. This gift is very closely related to the word of knowledge, insofar as it may be an impression upon one's mind or a thought brought to one's mind by the Holy Spirit, as we are yielded to Him.

The basis for operating in any of the gifts is faith in Jesus Christ. As we move in that faith in Him, the Holy Spirit can move through us and the gifts of the Spirit be clearly manifested. When we ask for these gifts in faith, nothing wavering, God will always grant our request.

EIGHT

Word of Knowledge

To another the word of knowledge (I Corinthians 12:8).

I believe that the word of knowledge is a thought, or impression on our mind or a vision or the direct audible voice of the Holy Spirit ABOUT a situation. This gift amazes and heartens people perhaps as greatly as the casting out of demons or the gifts of healing. But far beyond that, it becomes a viable channel to bring restoration to needy people.

In the flesh, I had been a greedy person. Praise God, when I came into the things of the Spirit I was greedy for God. I said to my heavenly Father, "Lord, I just want *all* of those gifts!" And over the years, in varying dimensions, I believe I have moved in all of them; this has been confirmed by other members of the body of Christ.

I came into the things of the Spirit under the ministry of a man who operated very freely in the word of knowledge. But the word of knowledge came to me only as the result of quite a long battle. (I do not suggest that your experience will be the same; many of you may already operate in this gift.) Here's how it happened. It was in that simple prayer meeting held in my home (again, through the love of that Pentecostal brother) that I began to move. He was moving freely in the gifts and was undergoing persecution because his church did not believe as he did in the things of the Spirit. I am glad to report that he remained faithful in that church, which today is fully charismatic.

This same man stood with me for nine months because I told him I wanted to move in the word of knowledge. He would have a tremendous word for thirty, forty or fifty people as he stood with them towards the end of the meeting. As I stood next to him, he would ask, "Brother Bill, do you hear anything from the Lord?" I would say, "No, nothing."

That happened the first week, the second week, the third week, the fourth week — thirty-five weeks in all. "Brother Bill, do you hear anything from the Lord?" I heard nothing!

I believe there are times God wants to show us that we must be persistent. Some, of course, can move more freely than others. I am seeing my own children moving straight into it without any difficulty.

But I had to persevere. One night during the thirty-sixth week, as I hung in there, the anointing came upon me and something was impressed upon my mind. I began to speak out concerning the person before me. Within moments the brother said, "Bill, that's from the Lord—I have the same word!" Once I received that impression upon my mind, I anticipated more of them. I waited expectantly week after week, until one night I began to hear *audibly* the voice of the Lord. I believe implicitly that phrase of John's in the Scriptures:

> ...*but whatsoever he shall hear, that shall he speak...* (John 16:13).

As the Holy Spirit hears from God, He speaks to us accordingly. It must be confirmed, of course, that it is the Holy Spirit speaking to a person. That is where our submission to the body of Christ is so vital.

There are people for whom I prayed for the baptism in the Spirit who were not open to the appropriate admonition, would not receive correction, and were not delivered from a spirit of deception. They have gone out and moved in the Spirit of God, and also moved in the spirit of deception—and I have *never* seen such confusion. They had the Holy Spirit but were subject to spiritual deception.

The last time I heard from one man to whom I saw this happen, he told me he was going to the most sothern part of South America to buy a motor car to drive to Canada, since God had told him to do so. He listened to nobody! So we need to be subject to the body of Christ.

Concerning the audible voice of the Lord, sometimes in a meeting it is totally audible to me. I have been in situations where , as I moved about in a meeting, I could hear the voice of the Lord very clearly telling me about conditions in people nearby, or some other situation. I would move into another place in the same meeting and could hear nothing. In this way I began to recognize how the Spirit of God can be quenched, perhaps by unbelief, in meetings.

I was walking down the aisle of a church in New Zealand, in a city called Dunedin, and about every three feet I would sense a blank. I could stand in one position, look along the rows, and hear the voice of the Holy Spirit telling me about a specific person in the row. I would call the individual out and the word given me would be absolutely right. I would move another three feet and not hear a thing. Another three feet, and the Holy Spirit would speak to me again.

I said to the vicar, "There is something wrong in this church." Then I began to spiritually discern five portals or frames along the church at intervals. They seemed to be in the construction of the building, but I saw them only in the spirit.

I shared this with the minister. "Oh, Bill," he said, "that's right. yes, there are five of those pillars—this building was erected by the Masonic Lodge."

"Well," I said, "brother, you know that the Masonic Lodge is demonic. You need to reconsecrate this church."

"We have done that," he replied.

Then he explained to me that a hundred years ago the Masons had walked down the main street of that city, shovels on their shoulders, to lay the foundations of that building.

Let me be clear: I love the Masons themselves but hate the occult spirit of freemasonry. Well, I prayed afresh with the vicar, in faith, by agreement, and we were settled within our hearts, but nothing seemed to happen at that time. Later that afternoon we were in a home praying for a sick person when suddenly the Spirit of God let me know, "That building is released"—and I felt in my spirit that it had happened.

God had heard the prayer which we had prayed. I went down to see the building, anxious to prove it. That night I preached, then began to move about, listening to the voice of the Lord. Sure enough, I could hear Him from one end of the church to the other. There was no longer any blank space as I moved around. I could hear His voice in every part of that church. God's Spirit was no longer being quenched.

I praise God for the fruit that comes forth when we belive His Spirit.

In the New Hebrides (now Vanuatu), I was taken by the bishop to a hospital, where he asked, "Will you pray for some of the sick people?" I had to speak at a meeting that night. tired, and realizing that once I entered I could not tell how long it would take, I was a little reluctant. As I prayed for these sick people, it was not difficult to know their problem; all in that ward were lepers. So I prayed a general prayer and prepared to leave.

Then the superintendent of the hospital saw me exercising the word of knowledge and, saying by way of explanation, "You believe you know what is wrong with people," asked me to come into the main ward.

As we entered he asked, "What is that patient suffering from?" Just like that!

Well, that's really testing you. He pulled the chart at the back of the bed, looked at it, and waited for me to answer. The Spirit of God told me, one after the other, of four problems from which the patient suffered. More than a little amazed, the superintendent, a very methodical man, ticked off those conditions. He went to the next bed. Exactly the same thing happened. We went to the next bed, and the next bed. By the time we reached the seventh, I had grown bolder. And so we moved to each of the thirty beds in that hospital. The God glorifying result of this demonstration was that the superintendent came that night to the meeting and was baptized in the Holy Spirit.

The voice of the Lord is a still, small voice. As we open ourselves to Him and begin to trust Him, even for impressions upon our minds, He is able to move. I began to move forward in this particular gift in a small prayer meeting—not the one in our home, but at my local church on a Sunday night—where there used to be nine or ten people. The Lord would impress upon me that somebody had a headache. "All right," I said, "somebody has a headache." Now, that is not a big thing, but somebody did have a headache, and it encouraged my faith. As I continued I would believe the Lord was speaking to me about somebody's kidneys: "I believe somebody has a kidney problem." And someone would answer, "Yes," and I would pray for them.

Then I began to learn that the Holy Spirit will also impress upon you conditions related to people other than those in the meeting. For example, when a person came with a concern for someone else, I learned that you may be given by the Holy Spirit an accurate description of that condition. While nobody in the meeting would have that condition, somebody would be there who had a burden for that person. I have seen many people healed when they began to understand that God is so wide in His love that He is concerned for *all* of our problems, not just for those people who are sitting at a meeting. If you are concerned about your family right now and what is happening within it, God may well be helping them even now, as you believe and are reading this. He is not limited by time or space.

Recently as I was giving this message at a Philadelphia meeting, a woman pastor who really wanted to move out in the gifts of the Holy Spirit began to believe for this gift. When I stopped the meeting for a short time so that people might greet one another, she turned around to speak to my daughter-in-law, seated immediately behind her. (The lady pastor did not know to whom she was speaking.) She said, "I believe I have a word of knowledge for you." For the first time in her life, she gave a word directly from the Lord, and very accurate. It related to a desire deep in the heart of my daughter-in-law. It was so astonishingly accurate that it shook both of them. How important it is to really believe for God's blessing! Then we will receive.

If you are close to and working with any person moving in the gifts of the Holy Spirit, I believe you will move very quickly yourself in the gifts of the Spirit. My own family have come into the gifts much more rapidly than I did, simply because on many occasions they have sat under my ministry and seen this gift operate.

We must be moving in faith. All gifts are based upon it. When I come to a meeting I may feel terrible, but as I seek the Lord Jesus Christ I begin to hear His voice or receive an impression upon my mind concerning the situation. I am not saying that I came into the experience overnight. I practiced the gift and it has grown within me.

As the Spirit of God moves across a meeting, an authority comes into that meeting, and you can begin to operate in that authority. You begin to hear His voice very clearly, as though a person were standing beside you, constantly talking to you. I have been in a meeting where the Lord accurately conveyed to me, one after another, specifics on all kinds of situations, I can only explain, as humbly as possible, exactly what He gives me.

It is important always to remember this verse from Hebrews:

> But Strong meat belongeth to them that are of full age, even those who by reason of use have their senses exercised to discern both good and evil (Hebrews 5:14).

It is important to utilize your human senses while functioning in the gifts of the Holy Spirit. We must continually be open and learn to grow in faith so that we may move more deeply into the gifts.

I learned that I must exercise the gifts of the Holy Spirit by going into situations where I had the opportunity for practice. That is what I did with the word of knowledge. I found it to be a tremendous gift in the ministry. If you are going into a town and praying with the word of knowledge, you will soon fill any hall. It is surely by the exercise of this gift, among others, that the early church manifested such power. It is a valid gift which every believer is entitled to seek.

An example of Jesus exercising the word of knowledge may be taken from John's gospel:

Jesus saith unto her, Go, call thy husband, and come hither. The woman answered and said, I have no husband. Jesus said unto her, Thou has well said, I have no husband:

For thou hast had five husbands; and he whom thou now hast is not thy husband: in that saidst thou truly.

The woman saith unto him, Sir, I perceive that thou art a prophet (John 4:16-19).

Jesus exercised the word of knowledge to show His supernatural power and wisdom at this time, and it was such a witness to this woman that she indeed believed He was the Messiah.

People have asked me, "Why should God allow us to read the thoughts and intents of other persons' hearts?" They cannot believe that this is of the Holy Spirit. However, if we look at the Scriptures we find that the word of knowledge as set out in I Corinthians 12 is part of the Word of God. Then, turning to the Epistle to the Hebrews, we find these words:

For the word of God is quick, and powerful, and sharper than any two-edged sword, piercing even to the dividing asunder of soul and spirit, and of the joints and marrow, and is a discerner of the thoughts and intents of the heart (Hebrews 4:12).

Here is a clear indication that the word of knowledge will allow us to discern the thoughts and intents of the heart of others in certain circumstances, as we operate under the anointing of the Holy Spirit.

In counseling it saves hours of time, since it takes you directly to the cause of a problem. It is important that you put all things completely out of your mind, other than the knowledge of Jesus Christ and His presence. As you do He is able to speak to you concerning the person whom you are counseling.

It is also very important to persevere when you believe you have received something from God. I have been to meetings where the Holy Spirit spoke to me about a person's condition which I was then able to describe with great accuracy, but where nobody responded. As I have continued to persevere, however, even for several minutes, someone finally has stood to his feet and said, "I believe it is me," and it has been, in fact, that person.

Many people after the meetings will come up and say, "We were embarrased and did not want to come out during the meeting." But when you hang in there the Spirit of God meets the situation. Hold on in faith—faith is one of the basic gifts in which we must move.

If I believe I have a word from God for a person, I hold to that word and I find that they come forward eventually.

If I stand at any meeting where the gospel is preached and begin to wait upon the Lord, I will hear His voice concerning people in that meeting. I am not boasting; I just expect it to happen. It is part of having an expectant faith as you work in the gifts. So I encourage you to *expect* the gifts to operate through you, and you will discover it happening.

Quite frequently when my wife is to speak at a meeting she will ask me ahead of time concerning any words of knowledge I may have received for that group. I give them to her, she lists them, and at the meeting describes the conditions, asking the persons concerned to stand. The Holy Spirit knows they are going to be there, and He has given the prior word of knowledge. This greatly increases faith at a meeting.

Often I wait upon the Lord before a meeting at which I am to speak, and He gives me accurate words of knowledge concerning people who will be there. I write these down and call them out at the meeting, especially if I am short of time, and because God knew they would be there and prepared their hearts, these people will come forward.

Yield to God and you will hear Him continually. The words in John 16:13 do not say that He speaks only between one and two o'clock in the morning, but at any time, and the more we yield to Him the more we will hear Him.

But remember that there are other voices in the world as well. That is why we must be committed to, and a part of, the body of Christ, where our gifts from the Lord may be tested and confirmed.

Summing up this gift therefore I repeat that I believe it is a thought, or an impression on our mind or a vision, or the direct audible voice from the Holy Spirit telling us about a situation.

NINE

Gift of Faith

To another faith by the same spirit . . . (I Corinthians 12:9).

Faith is a gift. It comes from total belief in the Word of God:

So then faith cometh by hearing, and hearing by the word of God (Romans 10:17).

It grows through constant reading of the Word and total belief in it. We must totally believe the Word of God without question, if faith is to grow. Each time I open the Bible, I ask the Lord for a *rhema*: that is, for a part of His Word to be specially enlivened to me; and He never fails. Faith comes from simple, childlike belief in the Word.

Faith must not be confused with feeling. Faith touches our spirit, while feeling springs from our soulish area — the emotions. Many times I have stood before a meeting feeling very sick, but, putting that aside, I have had faith in the Word. Then as I ministered in faith, I have felt the presence of God.

Some people mistakenly try to feel the presence of God in

order to obtain faith — but He wants us to move in faith first. Then feeling follows.

Some men have great faith to see people healed of ear problems, others have great faith for people who need their teeth filled. It's just a particular dimension of faith with which God has blessed them as they seek to expand in that area.

I have a strong gift of faith, for example, for people's back conditions, for asthma or diabetes or similar conditions, perhaps more than in some other areas of human need.

I believe that as you go from faith to faith you can see people healed in greater and greater measure. It is a great way in which to pray for people. You build faith upon faith; so from a very practical point of view if you want to move in the gift of faith, build upon the faith which God has already given you. Maybe you will start in a simple area of healing. Just continue to believe and as you do you will grow in that area.

We should be prepared to move in the faith that God offers us, not limiting Him. And always remember that faith is a gift also to the person for whom you are praying. Through the Word of God the gift of faith may be implanted in a person's heart, and just at that moment tremendous healing can begin or be accomplished. So never overlook the need for faith in that person.

If we believe implicitly that —

. . . *they shall lay hands on the sick, and they shall recover* (Mark 16:18),

their recovery starts immediately. This is an act of faith, even though nothing may appear to happen at that time.

One of the circumstances in which the enemy attacks is when we are tired; in that state we may find it difficult to move in the area of faith.

Faith is based upon an implicit trust in the Word of God, and He is able to pour out a richer measure of faith as we believe the Word. Remember, of course:

> *For verily I say unto you. That whosoever shall say unto this mountain, Be thou removed, and be thou cast into the sea; and shall not doubt in his heart, but shall believe that those things which he saith shall come to pass; he shall have whatsoever he saith* (Mark 11:23).

If we begin to verbalize wrong attitudes and thoughts, then we receive those attitudes and thoughts because our ears hear what our mouth speaks out. This is a faith destroyer. Instead, our faith can be fortified if we are prepared to praise God, no matter what the circumstances.

There have been so many times when events were working totally against me, and I have gone into my office, knelt and praised God, believing He was in charge of the situation. As this measure of faith has been exercised despite how I have felt, the circumstances which I thought were traumatic have fallen away and a beautiful solution has been found for the problem.

I have mentioned the need for complete and absolute faith in the Word of God. It is the foundation of all faith: complete, unquestioning belief (as a little child) that the Bible is the Word of God. I discover that many people have difficulty in reading and understanding the Word because their mind gets in the way. The greatest enemy of faith is unbelief. If we persist in unbelief long enough, the spirit of unbelief enters. It is remarkable how, when we entertain unbelief, thoughts can lodge in our minds and remain there long after we have forgotten them, ready to rise up when we wish to move in faith.

I remember reading a footnote to a certain translation of Mark 16 in the Bible. It stated that the latter part of Mark 16 did not appear in the original manuscripts. This created doubt in my mind concerning the statements of Jesus about healing and casting out of devils, until I realized that whether or not those verses were in the original, we read in the Book of Acts of these things happening after Pentecost. However, the thought still remained in my mind and would surface periodically.

Subsequently I found that there are 4,200 Greek manuscripts of the New Testament. At least 680 of them contain the Gospel of Mark, and only two of these 680 do not have these verses. Of three Latin versions, 8,000 now exist — and they all contain the verses in question. The Gothic versions, the Egyptian versions and the Armenian versions all contain these verses.

It was not until the fourth century that the verses were questioned. In one of the two oldest versions in which they are missing, there is a space left blank, apparently for these verses; and in the other manuscript also ommitted are Genesis 1-46, Psalms 105-137, Hebrews 9:14 and 13:25, all of Timothy 1 and 2, Titus, Philemon and Revelation!

Of course, it was very comforting to read these facts. Nevertheless, the belief which had entered through my reading that faith-inhibiting footnote took a lot of erasing.

Similarly, when we seek to move in faith all kinds of factors around us can intrude. It may be our education, our training in a particular discipline, or our reliance on man. For example, I have found that doctors readily believe in the power of God to heal, yet nurses, so accustomed to relying upon the skill of doctors, often have difficulty in relying upon God's Word.

For these reasons I encourage people to renounce any spirit of unbelief. This spirit can be particularly strong if they are involved in the occult or if their parents have been involved in the occult. A familiar spirit can then come down through generations to bind that person's mind.

When individuals say they have difficulty in reading the Bible and understanding it, or that a veil seems to come over them when they attempt to read the Bible, I look upon it as a possible indication that they have been involved in the occult and need deliverance.

Faith is a finely balanced, tender plant needing to be nurtured. If we rely totally upon our natural mind we shall not operate in faith. We must understand the spiritual dimension. As Paul writes,

> *While we look not at the things which are seen, but at the things which are not seen: for the things which are seen are temporal; but the things which are not seen are eternal* (II Corinthians 4:18).

We should be aware of the spiritual dimension around us, the two kingdoms — of God and of Satan. We will only come into spiritual understanding as we approach the Word of God with the simplicity of a little child.

For all these reasons, if we are going to operate in faith we must nurture the faith which God has given us in His Word. We must come to the Word totally believing and accepting what it says to us.

I never question the Word of God. If I do not understand it, I just believe it. Then in time the Holy Spirit shows me clearly what is meant by a particular phrase or portion of it. To our natural minds the Word of God may at times seem to contradict itself, but once we move in the Spirit we can see clearly that there is no contradiction in any part of the Word of God. The failure of our natural minds to grasp the spiritual insights which God offers is what prevents our understanding of the Word.

Thus God offers us this gift of faith, and we are to receive it without question or argument. As we continue to exercise it, we begin to sense God's wonderful anointing upon it.

One word which has always been a tremendous encouragement to me is found in Matthew, where Jesus said,

> . . . *All power is given unto me in heaven and in earth* (Matthew 28:18).

That word *power* means authority.

> *Go ye therefore, and teach all nations, baptizing them in the name of the Father, and of the Son, and of the Holy Ghost:*
> *Teaching them to observe all things whatsoever I have commanded you: and, lo, I am with you alway, even unto the end of the world* (Matthew 28:19,20).

As Jesus has given us His authority, we can command healings and deliverance in His name, acting in faith. But it has been the Word illuminated to us, the *rhema*, which has given us that faith in which to operate.

We must be disciplined in the Word of God if we are to go in faith. We must study the Word diligently, making it our first priority of the day, if we are going to really grow in it. If we cannot accomplish it early in the day, then we must find some definite time each day to read it.

Our spirit must be fed. Our natural body is fed with food and our mind is fed with what we read and hear and see. Our spirit, if we are committed to Jesus Christ, is fed only from the Word of God.

If we are prepared to act in this way, yielding to God through His Spirit as we read the Word, then the gift of faith grows. We pray in accordance with the Word, we believe the Word, we do not doubt the Word. Then it works.

> *Is not my word like as a fire? saith the Lord; and like a hammer that breaketh the rock in pieces?* (Jeremiah 23:29).

TEN

Gifts of Healing

. . . to another the gifts of healing by the same Spirit (I Corinthians 12:9).

If you implicitly believe the verses from Mark 16 where it says that if you lay hands on the sick they shall recover, recovery starts immediately.

. . . they shall lay hands on the sick, and they shall recover (Mark 16:18).

I believe that every person for whom I pray and upon whom I lay hands begins to be healed immediately. If the healing has not already started before that, it begins at that point. There are no exceptions. To lay hands on the sick and to believe for their healing is a scriptural method for being healed. And I believe that the healing begins immediately.

Among other reasons, healing may be blocked by sin or unforgiveness on the part of a person. Many times as I have ministered to a person the Holy Spirit has quickened to me that there is unforgiveness in that person's heart. The Spirit of God is endeavouring to touch and to heal him but the hardness is blocking what God wants to do.

As a sovereign God, He will move in any circumstance or situation. I don't want to set out a list of rules for healing, but I do want to tell you that forgiveness (a basic pre-requisite to expressing love) is a basic requirement for healing.

I have asked people to stand in a church and begin to forgive. I have asked them to name those whom they should forgive. The pastor has come to me and said. "Brother, some people are offended because you made them do it three times." That same pastor has come to me a year later, reporting an elderly man in his church healed instantly of arthritis (which he had had for thirty years) as he began to forgive his son.

From the moment I began to move in the ministry of healing, and in the prayer of faith for healing, with the word of knowledge, I found the Lord impressing upon my mind the need for people to forgive; for men to honour their parents, to understand that they are accepted by God, that they are accepted in the Beloved:

> *To the praise of the glory of his grace, wherein he hath made us accepted in the beloved* (Ephesians 1:6).

When people can begin to understand that they are truly accepted by God, that they are forgiven, and that they must forgive, a release takes place. So in praying for the sick it is essential that we obey the Word of God. Based on Isaiah 59:1,2, I believe that where there is unbelief and a spirit of unforgiveness or other sin, it can block His healing power.

Other sins can prevent healing. I know of a girl, age fourteen, who had leukemia. The doctors had given up; they said she had only a few hours to live. I went to pray for her, and as I entered the room all the family were there, grouped around her. As I stood there the Lord began to speak to me about her father: "This man has been fornicating for the last ten years." That shook me.

I prayed for the girl, then went outside and began to speak to the father about how the Lord was able to heal and save. He responded to me by saying, "I'd like to believe you, Bill, but I have problems in my life."

I did not tell him I already knew of his problems. Instead I asked. "What is your problem?"

He answered, "I just can't stop chasing other women."

I have seen that girl since — she has improved remarkably. Her father made a partial repentance, but later went back to his former condition. He said, "I prefer to carry on the way I am." I told him, "The healing for your child is greatly dependent upon your attitude in this matter." He would not give it up even for his child. However, the mother continued to believe, and I saw that child, considerably improved, a year later at a meeting. But I believe there was a direct spiritual link — not in all cases, but in that case — between the sins of the father and the daughter's illness.

(That is the third child I have prayed for who suffered from leukemia whose father had been fornicating).

It is important that in healing we encourage people to thank God *before* they see the healing manifested in their body. This is faith in accordance with Mark:

> *Therefore I say unto you. What things soever ye desire, when ye pray, believe that ye receive them, and ye shall have them* (Mark 11:24).

I always encourage people to believe they have received their healing, although they may feel nothing at the initial stage. Often I have returned to places a year or two later, to learn that many were completely healed over a period of time after the first meeting.

When I am praying for a sick person I stand quietly with him, centre my thoughts on Jesus Christ, then begin to sense the anointing of the Spirit descending. I try to keep a humble attitude, with total dependency upon the Lord Jesus Christ, and as I am able to do so I find that His power and love operate in the most impossible situations.

In order to operate with the gift of faith for healing and in the gift of healing, I must be absolutely singleminded, believing in the authority that is given me by the Word of God to His servants:

> *They shall take up serpents; and if they drink any deadly thing, it shall not hurt them; they shall lay hands on the sick, and they shall recover* (Mark 16:18).

I recently had the experience of praying with a lady of eighty years who was almost entirely deaf. She had written, asking that I pray for her. I responded that I would be happy to do so, provided her vicar was present (she had told me she was a churchgoer). Her vicar called me by telephone, saying that he would be happy if I should pray for his parishioner. Nevertheless, he was concerned that if she were not healed she might lose her faith. Obviously, this man had reservations concerning the power of God to heal under these circumstances.

As he and I walked together to this lady's home, I shared with him the words that "with God nothing is impossible." He agreed.

We entered the lady's home to find a parishioner friend, seventy-five years old and partly deaf, present with her. Although the lady used a hearing aid, she was so deaf that I had to shout at the top of my voice, speaking very slowly, in order for her to understand what I was saying. It was clear from the outset that she loved the Lord Jesus Christ and had faith in her heart, but it was also clear that she couldn't hear anything.

After offering counsel concerning the ability of the Lord Jesus Christ to heal, and His gift of healing for her, I asked the vicar to anoint her with oil, which he did. Then I laid hands upon her, praying for her healing, and immediately I sensed the presence of the Holy Spirit.

After praying, I spoke no more to her but turned my attention to her seventy-five-year-old lady friend, who appeared to have an improvement in her hearing as soon as we had prayed for her.

I then turned again to the eighty-year-old, temporarily forgetting that previously I had had to shout. I spoke to her in a normal voice. She responded immediately, hearing me clearly. The longer our conversation continued, the more astonished the vicar became. God had performed a miracle in a moment, and this dear lady was able to hear in a beautiful and normal manner.

In ministering healing to the sick, it is most important that God's love also be ministered. If the sick person feels you are judging him for past sin in his life, or in respect to any other matter in his heart, he will shrink back from the fullness of God's power which should be operating through you.

When we minister to the sick, we must accept people as they are. They need to be told that they are loved and accepted by God. We all need to understand that God accepts and loves us, and as we do so we can accept His healing love and power much more deeply.

I find so many people are rejected, and suffer from feelings of rejection, particularly if there has been wrong parental relationship or unforgiveness in their lives. As they are encouraged to honour their parents and forgive others, and as the love of God flows through you as the ministering person, the healing power and the anointing of God may fall upon them.

Praying for the sick is not a mechanical action. It is an act of love, and it requires the total giving of oneself by the person who is praying. If we are to be ministers of God's love, then we must act in love.

It is good to speak the Word of God to a sick person and to encourage him by pointing out that Christ indeed died not only to give him the gift of eternal life and to forgive him of all sins, but also to heal him:

. . . by whose stripes ye were healed (I Peter 2:24).

In praying for the person to be healed, I wait upon the Lord until I sense the power of the Holy Spirit upon me. This usually comes in the form of the anointing — but not always. I try to set my heart at peace before God and focus my whole mind upon Him. With total belief in my heart, I recall the promises of God and, having counselled the person to release any bitterness, unforgiveness, rejection or fear, I can then believe for God's Spirit to touch that person. As I said earlier, the sick person must believe that God has touched him and must begin to praise Him for the healing, although there may be no immediate evidence in his body.

The ministry of healing requires sacrifice on our part. We are often approached to pray for the sick when it is not very convenient for us. We may be required to travel considerable distances; people may come to our home at an inconvenient hour; they may telephone us at a late hour of the evening. All of this requires the fruit of love and patience in our lives combined with a sense of complete dedication.

When praying for the sick, we must never overlook the admonition from James:

> *Is any sick among you? let him call for the elders of the church; and let them pray over him, anointing him with oil in the name of the Lord* (James 5:14).

Usually prayer for the sick is best carried out in the presence of a group of believing elders from the church. For this reason, I always ask whether or not the elders of the person's church have already prayed for him. We must always encourage believers to look in the first place for ministry to their own pastor and elders. If the person persists, then I will usually ask whether their pastor or elders can be present when I pray for them.

On the other hand, there are many circumstances when it is not practicably to suggest such a course of action. Sometimes the person does not belong to a church, or it is an emergency situation and the church is a very considerable distance away. In all of these circumstances every Christian should be prepared to minister in love to the sick, acting in faith, in accordance with the Word of God.

ELEVEN

Miracles

To another the working of miracles (I Corinthians 12:10).

The gift of miracles is often reflected in instantaneous healing. Observe how Jesus healed the nobleman's son:

> When he heard that Jesus was come out of Judaea into Galilee, he went unto him, and besought him that he would come down, and heal his son: for he was at the point of death.
>
> Then said Jesus unto him, Except ye see signs and wonders, ye will not believe.
>
> The nobleman saith unto him, Sir, come down ere my child die.
>
> Jesus saith unto him, Go thy way; thy son liveth. And the man believed the word that Jesus had spoken unto him, and he went his way.
>
> And as he was now going down, his servants met him, and told him, saying, Thy son liveth.
>
> Then inquired he of them the hour when he began to amend. And they said unto him, Yesterday at the seventh hour the fever left him.

> So the father knew that it was at the same hour, in the which
> Jesus said unto him, Thy son liveth: and himself believed, and his
> whole house.
> This is again the second miracle that Jesus did, when he was
> come out of Judaea into Galilee (John 4:47-54).

This is described as the second *miracle* which Jesus performed; thus, an instantaneous healing is properly referred to as a miracle.

When I say that as we lay hands on the sick they begin to recover, I have no doubt about it. On some occasions, however, the Spirit of God moves miraculously on people, we see the electricity of God pulsing through their bodies, and there may be an instantaneous healing. So we do not limit God either way, for He does bestow the gift of miracles.

Let us believe Him for miracles, and let us not be discouraged. And if we do not see instantaneous miracles, let us keep a balance in the Word of God; let us not go back into unbelief and say that God does not heal.

We must always remember that as we lay hands on the sick they shall *recover*, and also that God is a God of *miracles*.

Let us also remember that Jesus told us,

> Verily, verily, I say unto you, He that believeth on me, the
> works that I do shall he do also; and greater works than these shall
> he do; because I go unto my Father (John 14:12)

God is not bound by time or circumstance. Contrary to the case in the natural realm, in the spiritual realm miracles are within our grasp if we only will move in that realm with total belief in our heart.

As always, of course, we must be obedient to the Word of God and insure that our requests are in accordance with His Word. If we have a right heart relationship towards Him, and are obeying the commandment of Jesus to love one another as He loved us, then I believe we are on strong ground for God's grace to operate in our lives. Remember, we are told.

And this is the confidence that we have in him, that, if we ask any thing according to his will, he heareth us (I John 5:14).

I've found it is generally easy to find the will of God because the Scriptures are so clear. It is obviously His will to *prosper* us in a total sense:

For ye know the grace of our Lord Jesus Christ, that though he was rich, yet for your sakes he became poor, that ye through his poverty might be rich (II Corinthians 8:9).

It is obviously God's will to give us *health* in a total sense:

Beloved, I wish above all things that thou mayest prosper and be in health, even as thy soul prospereth (III John 2).

Who his own self bare our sins in his own body on the tree, that we, being dead to sins, should live unto righteousness: by whose stripes ye were healed (I Peter 2:24).

I recall an incident a few years ago in a city in New Zealand were I was speaking at a Women's Aglow meeting. After I had finished, the Holy Spirit directed my attention to a person present who He let me know had wanted to have a child for the last seven years. The Spirit revealed to me that her womb was twisted, almost into an inverted position.

As I spoke the words the Holy Spirit gave me, a young lady rushed forward. She knew the Holy Spirit was speaking about her. As I began to pray for her, she fell to the floor under the power of the Spirit. As we watched, we observed her abdominal area moving up and down in a great heaving motion. She seemed to be in some pain, but it was clear to me that the power of God was moving through her body. Then she jumped to her feet and said, "I know I am healed!"

God had reversed the womb condition in a moment of time, as she had touched the hem of His garment. A few months later she was pregnant. A year later we visited that same city and she brought her child to the public meeting and gladly gave her testimony to the glory of God.

In these areas of healing and many others, as we remain humble before the Lord and believe His Word, He is able to accomplish miracles.

TWELVE

Prophecy

. . . to another prophecy (I Corinthians 12:10).

I believe that the gift of prophecy is exercised when we open our hearts and minds to God. He can give us an impression or a thought or a vision or we can hear His direct audible voice and as we trust God and believe it is Him then others in the body of Christ will discern that indeed we are speaking a word from the Lord.

I believe every person should prophesy in accordance with I Corinthians:

> *For ye may all prophesy one by one, that all may learn, and all may be comforted (I Corinthians 14:31).*

Every Spirit-filled believer should have the gift of prophecy. At meetings, I sometimes ask the gathering to stand and those who have never prophesied to wait quietly upon the Lord, letting Him bring Bible verses or some words to their mind. I usually ask others to lay hands on those who wish to prophesy by the Spirit of God, because people need to practice their gift.

If you want to move in prophecy, I suggest you join a group that will love you, I'm not talking about leaving your church; I'm referring to a prayer-meeting situation where people will love you and accommodate your desire to move in this dimension.

As words come into your mind, speak them out. (I mean words that are for edification, exhortation and comfort.) Frequently I ask people to quote Bible verses so that they may hear their own voice. Once you have heard your voice in an open meeting you begin to gain confidence and faith.

It is important that you make a start. You may have only a few words, but if you reach out in faith, speak those words. Do not wait until you get the whole message. Just bring forth what you believe is being said to you, then you may stop. You may have nothing further to say and somebody else may bring the rest of the prophecy.

You grow in faith only by speaking good words out of your mouth. We all know that. I was very shy when I first became a Christian and very impressed by the confidence of people who prophesied. Then I began to realize that all God wanted me to do was to remain as a child, relying upon Him. One day I was encouraged by a brother to do just that. He encouraged those in the gathering to speak out a simple word. I spoke a few words of a psalm, and as soon as I heard my voice in the open prayer meeting I began to gain confidence. I started to move from then on. It just flows as we stand with a person for prayer. The Lord is always willing to give a word.

> For ye may all prophesy one by one, that all may learn, and
> all may be comforted (I Corinthians 14:31).

Prophecy is also for edification, exhortation and comfort:

> But he that prophesieth speaketh unto men to edification, and
> exhortation, and comfort (I Corinthians 14:2)

It is to edify and to build up the body of Christ.

The leader has a significant responsibility in leading a prayer meeting. If he is gifted in the area of prophecy, he must listen carefully to the Lord, for the Lord often wants to bring a simple word of encouragement.

Remember that the gift of prophecy is different from the ministry of a prophet; that is another ministry (Ephesians 4:11). We are talking about the ministry of prophecy, not prophesying future events so much as building up the body of Christ. All of the gifts are for the purpose of edification.

When we started our prayer meetings, the Holy Spirit laid it upon my heart to encourage my wife. She would be in the meeting and I would say, "I believe the Lord is giving you a word, Pat." (There were people present who could prophesy very well, while she had never done so; but standing firm in the Lord and in the faith God was implanting within her heart, she began to speak out.) Then steadily, word by word, it came. I have seen my wife at a meeting with 5,000 people, and the Lord would give her a prophecy that boomed right across the gathering as she spoke out. Many times as our family prays together the Lord gives my wife a word of encouragement. It's a wonderful and positive communication between husband and wife. So I say to you, encourage your wife, your husband, and your family to exercise this wonderful gift. It is a beautiful way in which God can reassure you.

My son Paul and my daughter Maria have this gift, too. It is a simple but beautiful gift of God. You begin by speaking out whatever God is laying on your heart. It may be, as I say, a psalm or a few words from the Scriptures, but speak it out. Do not be afraid to act, but get into a loving situation where you, too, can be blessed.

I praise God for showing me how to get started and for continuing to encourage me.

Do not overlook the fact that prophecy is often for *you*. While you are giving the word of prophecy, it may relate to your own circumstance and your own situation. God himself may be speaking to you as you speak the word.

Remember that the Holy Spirit does not interrupt Himself. If a message is being brought in tongues or interpretation, or in prophecy, then it should not be interrupted by another message coming at the same time. Sometimes this cannot be avoided in large meetings, where one person cannot hear what another is saying some distance away; but normally the Holy Spirit sorts that our fairly quickly and the voice of one person finally predominates.

When a prophecy is shared there should be a witness in the spirit of others that it is of God. Whether brought in English or through a tongue and interpretation, the Holy Spirit will show others in the meeting that it is a word of prophecy and of the Holy Spirit. If we do not have a witness to it and if it is not in accordance with the Word of God, then it should not be accepted.

Let the prophets speak two or three, and let the other judge (I *Corinthians* 14:29).

On the other hand, this must all be done in love. We would not shout a person down simply because they were bringing a word from their own mind rather than from the Spirit; the word may be perfectly harmless and yet uplifting. Judging (testing by the Word and Spirit) must surely be in love. But it must also be strong when the nature of the word given is directive, very condemnatory, or when it could bring some person into bondage.

If somebody else is speaking and we feel we have a tremendous burden to bring a word of prophecy or a message in a tongue, we should be prepared to wait until they finish and the opportunity opens up to bring that message. Some good folk have told me that they cannot hold the message God is giving them because they are bursting with it and *must* bring it. The Holy Spirit is a gentleman. He does not interrupt Himself, and He does not force Himself upon us. We should expect to have perfect control as we move in the Spirit. The Holy Spirit many times has given me a word of knowledge as somebody else was speaking. I do not jump up and say I want to bring that word right while some other person is bringing a message. I must wait until an appropriate opportunity presents itself.

It may be that I myself am speaking when the Holy Spirit brings me a word of knowledge, but still I wait until He shows me the right opportunity to bring that word.

And the spirits of the prophets are subject to the prophets (I*Corinthians* 14:32)

We should be able to exercise self-control.

If the leader of the meeting moves sensitively in the Spirit, he will sense that there is a word or message to be brought, and will help give the opportunity for it at the correct time.

Another way in which the gift of prophecy frequently operates is that the Holy Spirit begins to give us a picture of a situation in our mind's eye. It may be a waterfall, a sunset, or a field or some other situation. The Holy Spirit then begins to speak to us about it. The Holy Spirit is able to bring a vivid message as we speak forth with the picture in our mind. Both Pat and I frequently receive a picture in our minds as we are about to bring a prophecy, and as we begin to give expression to it we find that the prophecy becomes clearer to us.

As I am speaking in prophecy I receive only a few words in advance at each moment, and as I continue the Holy Spirit provides the words for speaking.

THIRTEEN

Gift of Discernment

. . . to another discerning of spirits (I Corinthians 12:10).

I believe that the gift of discernment can best be described as a thought, an impression or a vision or the direct audible voice of God telling us about spirits which are attacking a person or are involved in a situation.

The gift of discernment of spirits is a vital one for Christian ministry. It is linked to the casting out of demons.

Do you know that Jesus never once commissioned His disciples to pray for the sick without also commissioning them to cast out devils?

The ministry of standing on the authority of the Word of God and believing it implicitly enough to use against demon power is, I believe, for every one of us. I am not saying the ministry of casting out devils is necessarily for every one of us, but the ministry of standing on God's Word and *believing it against demon power* is for every one of us.

One night a brother at my prayer meeting said to me,

"Brother, the Lord is giving you the gift of discernment," I thank God for this brother who encouraged me in that way. From then on I began, by practice, to develop in the Lord's gift. As I prayed with people I found that the Holy Spirit would show me the various demons or spirits that controlled some of them, and so I began to move in considerable depth in this particular ministry.

However, a balance is needed. But I learned one thing which I have never forgotten. That is that I can take any verse from the Word of God — *any* verse — and speak it to someone who has a demon-problem and, as the demon manifests, it will invariably say, "I don't want to hear it, I don't want to hear it — I *do not* want to hear it!"

This is one more evidence of the authenticity of the Word of God. When you discern spirits and pray, you must have a complete faith within your heart. If you do not, you will be challenged by the demon before you.

I love to quote the Scriptures from Revelation:

> *And death and hell were cast into the lake of fire. This is the second death (Revelation 20:14).*

I tell the demon that is where it is going.

In Fiji a pastor and I were praying for a young couple. The girl received the baptism in the Spirit beautifully, but the young man was having considerable problems. The Holy Spirit had revealed to me there was still a Hindu spirit to be dealt with in his life. As we continued to pray, the people in the church, who knew we were ministering, began to sing. After awhile we heard them singing, "In the name of Jesus the demons must flee." As they sang this with great gusto, the young man began to sway backward and forward and a voice came from his mouth, singing the same tune. I knew it was not the boy; I knew it was a spirit.

I asked, "What on earth are you doing?"

The spirit replied, "This is my favourite tune."

Now, I know we are not supposed to converse at any length with demons, nor do I make a practice of it. But this is what that spirit said to me: "This is my favourite tune — in the name of Jesus the demons must flee." Then the realisation flooded over me that this demon had heard so many unbelieving Christians sing "In the name of Jesus the demons must flee" that he was no longer afraid, and had even made it his favourite tune. We must have faith in what we are doing!

The demon named himself — he was the Fijian shark god — and the young man was totally delivered, in the name of Jesus.

I report this to emphasize the need for proper spiritual discernment in these ministries. Even the devils believe in God, according to James 2:19. But accepting Jesus Christ as Lord and Saviour is an entirely different level of spiritual commitment. A total Christ-centred faith at work, based on the Word, is absolutely necessary in the discerning of spirits.

The discerning of spirits is a gift whereby the Holy Spirit clearly begins to create an uneasiness within you concerning a situation. As you wait upon the Lord you realise that there is a spirit of fear, rejection, or some other force operating in a person. Then there is, of course, a need for deliverance ministry.

The following is an example from the Scriptures concerning the use of this gift:

And it came to pass, as we went to prayer, a certain damsel possessed with a spirit of divination met us, which brought her masters much gain by soothsaying:

The same followed Paul and us, and cried, saying, These men are the servants of the most high God, which shew unto us the way of salvation.

And this did she many days. But Paul, being grieved, turned and said to the spirit, I command thee in the name of Jesus Christ to come out of her. And he came out the same hour (Acts 16:16-18).

Paul discerned a spirit of divination within the girl. Many times as we stand with a sick person we discern that the sickness is caused by a demonic force. As mentioned, Jesus never once commissioned His disciples to pray for the sick without commissioning them to cast out demons. The discerning of spirits is an important part of the healing ministry.

Often when people have harbored bitterness against others, even though they have forgiven them, the spirit of bitterness still remains attached to their being. A person may have repented of the bitterness but the spirit of bitterness itself may still be present, causing some physical problems. As the Holy Spirit reveals it, I command the spirit of bitterness to leave, and if the person remains in an attitude of repentance the spirit goes and the healing commences. This is particularly important in the case of arthritis and similar conditions.

When we are actually involved in deliverance ministry the discerning of spirits is valuable in discerning the chief demon and also whether the "cleansing of the house" (the person) has taken place. The Holy Spirit will bring to our mind through the gift of discernment the names of the various demons that may be involved with the person, and as they are named the demons will manifest themselves.

I well recall a man, approximately forty and a pillar in his church, was brought to me who claimed to be a tongues-speaking Christian, baptised in the Spirit, and leader of his prayer meeting. He told me that whenever he was leading his group something seemed to take over his voice and he would sing notes at an ever higher pitch.

As I waited upon the Lord, the Holy Spirit showed me that his mother had tried to abort him. I commanded the spirit of abortion to leave him, and this man lay upon the ground, curled up like a fetus, with the demon of abortion screaming out of him. As he was released from this demon, other demons also came out, until he was finally completely cleansed.

At times, demons do oppress Christian people and organisations. Under the authority of Anglican Bishop Chiu of Singapore, I was leading a teaching session with some of his clergy. During the course of the discussion the bishop, who is a godly and gentle man, said he believed the cathedral could be subject to demonic attack. Earlier, as I was speaking, I had discerned this, but had not felt it was my place to raise the issue.

As the bishop spoke to me I saw in my spirit the angel of death, three metres high, resting over the cathedral. I told the bishop about this, and he said, "Bill, I have no difficulty believing what you are saying. During the war years the Japanese took all the Australian nurses in Singapore, brought them into the grounds of this cathedral, and massacred them here. Their bodies were buried in these grounds and exhumed after the war."

With that we agreed to go outside and march around the cathedral, taking it Jericho style. As we passed the place where the girls had been buried I felt the anointing of God upon us, and as we trusted God I sensed the angel of death leaving the pinnacle of the cathedral and being brought down by the Spirit of God. We all sensed a tremendous anointing as the yoke of the enemy was broken, followed by great rejoicing.

When I pray for people with cancer I often discern a spirit of fear about them. Before I rebuke the spirit of cancer I command the spirit of fear to leave that person, and as they themselves renounce it in the name of Jesus, the Holy Spirit is able to touch and to deal with the remaining spirit of cancer.

To sum up, in order to operate in the gift of discerning of spirits we must yield our heart and mind to the Spirit of God. As we do so, He will quicken an uneasiness in our spirit and bring a thought or impression to our mind, and as we speak it out in faith we will find that the Holy Spirit confirms it.

The Holy Spirit often will show me that a person has been fornicating or is masturbating and I will take them aside and confront them about it. Sometimes they deny it at first, but then, feeling convicted, they admit it. As they confess these sins and renounce them, we command the spirit of fornication or the spirit of masturbation to leave, they are set free.

Masturbation, if allowed to control our body, brings with it other unclean habits and desires which we cannot control

We must always be aware that we are operating in the spiritual realm and against spiritual forces. God gives us the gift of discerning of spirts to enable us to discern the hand of the enemy and to set the captives free. If you are with a group of loving Christians and practicing this gift, as you let the Spirit of God impress something upon your heart or mind concerning a situation, you will discern any spirits that may be afflicting or tormenting any person present in the gathering. The Holy Spirit will bring to your mind the name of that spirit and, as you are all moving in openness and love, the person afflicted by that spirit will readily agree that this is so. Of course, sensitivity and wisdom must be observed.

Remember that even though we may have yielded our bodies as instruments of righteousness, in accordance with Romans 6:13, and have really turned to the Lord, these spirits can still be oppressing us, causing sickness, or seeking to torment us.

That is why the Holy Spirit has placed the gift of discernment and the ministry of deliverance in the body of Christ —so that we may defeat the darts of the enemy.

FOURTEEN

Tongues

. . . to another divers kinds of tongues (I Corinthians 12:10).

The gift of tongues for public ministry is a beautiful gift, and it too should edify the body of Christ.

Paul says,

> *I would that ye all spake with tongues, but rather that ye prophesied: for greater is he that prophesieth than he that speaketh with tongues, except he interpret, that the church may receive edifying* (I Corinthians 14:5).

It is therefore important that an interpreter be present when the message is brought in tongues, as otherwise there will be confusion. Paul says,

> *If any man speak in an unknown tongue, let it be by two, or at the most by three, and that by course; and let one interpret.*
> *But if there be no interpreter, let him keep silence in the church; and let him speak to himself, and to God* (I Corinthians 14:27,28).

It is therefore important that messages in tongues be delivered in order, and only one at a time, with at least one person present to interpret. Scripturally, it seems to me that there should be only two or three messages at the most in tongues in any one meeting.

Here again, encouragement is needed in speaking out in tongues. If we are prepared to put aside the thoughts of our natural mind and really center them on Jesus Christ in order to allow Him to speak to us, we will feel a quickening in our spirit that we should speak out in this way. We may have only the first few syllables to speak, but as we do God will anoint us with a message, and as the meeting is led by the Holy Spirit the interpretation will come. It may be from the person bringing the message, or it may be from another person.

As I began to lead our own prayer meetings the Holy Spirit spoke to me concerning the fact that He had given a person present among us a song. I began to encourage a certain lady to whom the Holy Spirit directed my attention in this regard, and as she began to sing in the Spirit, the anointing came upon her words. The Holy Spirit then gave clear direction that there were second and third verses. Finally the Holy Spirit gave me the faith to encourage my sister to bring the interpretation in English. This she did, in perfect rhythm and syllables, and as a result the meeting was greatly blessed. After being thus encouraged, this lady began to minister at other meetings and now has a tremendous ministry along these lines.

I was recently at a meeting of young Christians, some only a few weeks old in the Lord, teaching on the gifts of the Spirit.

I encouraged some of them to speak out in a new language which the Lord had given them. I waited on each occasion for the interpretation. The first message in tongues was rather hesitant and consisted of a few syllables only, but as boldness came upon the person the anointing began to fall. Almost immediately afterward a beautiful interpretation in English was presented. The person bringing the interpretation was a young man who had previously led a life of deep sin before coming to the Lord, but the anointing was unquestionably upon him.

The pastor of the church shook his head in disbelief. Although Spirit-filled, he found it difficult, as did others, to believe that God could move so spontaneously through such a new creature in Him. No, we do not need to be people of great learning or of great merit to operate in the gifts. We simply must believe the Lord and be faithful to what He gives us.

If you believe that the Lord wishes you to move in this gift, it is suggested you pray quietly in the Spirit so that no other person can hear you. Then as the opportunity offers itself and you believe it is God's will, bring forth the message in a tongue. Here again, it is wonderful to move in the confines of a small, loving prayer group which can assist you in developing this gift. You may only utter a few stammering syllables in tongues, but it will be a start. Encouragement in the gifts of the Spirit is indispensable if great growth is to result in this area. The love and concern of those around us can cause the flower of faith and love to bud and flourish abundantly in our midst.

I believe it is plain that the foregoing Bible passages are primarily for the public ministry of the gift of tongues; that is,

God impresses you to bring a word of prophecy in an unknown tongue. Most folk in this situation have a sense of God's anointing as they bring the message publicly. It is a public expression. The message comes in that tongue; then, of course, there should be the interpretation. We are told that at meetings there should be only three such messages. I don't know how legalistic we need to be, but that is what Paul seems to say in I Corinthians 14. (Otherwise, you could go on with tongue messages all night.) I take the view that, in addition, there should be an interpretation after each message. Otherwise, there could be confusion. So interpretation may come from the person bringing the message, or it may come from another person. Here again, it is a question of simply waiting upon God and trusting Him. If you believe He is speaking to you, then speak out according to His direction.

Sometimes when people move in this gift, they utter only a few syllables and then stop. They should be motivated by others to continue further; then God will anoint them. If the message is continually repetitive, using the same syllables, then obviously we must offer a gentle word of encouragement to insure that they go on to other words which God would have them speak.

FIFTEEN

Interpretation of Tongues

. . . to another the interpretation of tongues (I Corinthians 12:10).

I believe that the interpretation of tongues can be described as a thought, impression, or a vision or the direct audible voice of God speaking to our heart and mind and giving us words that interpret a message which has already been brought to us in a meeting through a tongue.

This gift may be exercised by means of encouragement within the body of Christ. After a message in a tongue has been brought, there should be a pause to enable the interpretation.

Here the leader of the meeting has a great responsibility to wisely aid the provision of an interpretation. Often God has given it to a person present at the meeting, and that person just needs a little motivation to bring forth the message.

We should remember that the interpretation of a tongue is not necessarily the *translation* of the message. People sometimes misunderstand, believing that it must be an exact literal translation of the message brought. But it is not a translation; it is an *interpretation*. However, I have known occasions when some person in the meeting who did not believe in the gifts of the Spirit was amazed to hear the message first in a language which he knew, then the interpretation, which was a perfect translation. God is not limited and the Spirit moves as He wills and to His glory. He may indeed bring a perfect translation through you or another person, but on the other hand it may be simply an interpretation of the truth presented.

I have heard some very young Christians bringing beautiful words of interpretation as they have moved in boldness. God wants bold people, and as we move in His boldness and love, if we are faithful and obedient to His Word, He will anoint us.

Speaking in tongues is really our spirit speaking to God with the aid of the Holy Spirit, right past our natural mind. I often encourage people who have spoken in a tongue to wait upon the Lord and follow it up with the English words that come into their mind. Many times this is a beautiful interpretation of what God has given them in the Spirit.

Prophecy and interpretation may be brought in any form of the native tongue. It does not have to be, for instance, in my language, King James English ('thus saith the Lord'), but can be brought in simple words of modern-day English. There are great messages delivered in large public meetings where God has anointed vessels to bring forward strong words of prophecy and interpretation in a very loud voice. Hearing these, some persons are intimidated, feeling themselves to be too weak a vessel to operate in this gift. We must not limit God to this form of ministry in a public meeting. He can just as easily operate in a small gathering of two or three persons with His still small voice, or in the largest meeting, speaking quietly through the most unassuming member of the group.

We must always be aware, in love one for another, that God may wish to speak through any Christian, bringing a message of great faith and hope to those nearby; in fact, often that person may be more spiritually attuned to what God is saying than the most "professional" prophet.

As we have discussed already under the gift of prophecy it is important to encourage people to move in this ministry of interpretation of tongues. Here again, we need to make a start and to trust God. As we are encouraged to do so then the Holy Spirit can speak through us and give the interpretation of a message which has already been brought in a tongue. These messages in tongues and their interpretation are often a form of prophecy and can be a message related both to the person bringing it or to the whole body of persons listening.

God loves to speak to His people. We only need to give Him the chance.

SIXTEEN

Leadership for the Meeting

It is very important that the leader of a meeting move sensitively in the Holy Spirit. We must be very attentive to God and to His voice.

So often, when singing and the praising of God have reached tremendous heights in the Spirit and God has wanted to bring a message, I have felt that the Holy Spirit has been grieved. Instead of waiting for that message, the leader of the meeting has plunged into the next song, whether it be praise or worship, and the opportunity has been lost. What is wrong with silence at the appropriate time? I am sure that some dear folk who are leading meetings feel that a moment of silence would be wrong, or perhaps they may even fear such a moment.

Again, some leaders appear to fear the move of the Spirit in a meeting. Perhaps they feel that some person may bring a wrong word of prophecy, or a word not anointed by the Spirit.

I have often been confronted with this situation. We must

remember that the word of prophecy or an interpretation can originate in the "soulish" realm; i.e., in the realm of the mind, not the realm of the spirit. It may be a perfectly good and valid word, but has arisen purely through the person's mind — not directly from inspiration of the Spirit. I do not go out of my way to stop such a word, because we can very easily damage the faith of some young Christian who is seeking to move in the Spirit. I would stop that person from speaking only when the word of prophecy or interpretation is contrary to the Word of God. In accordance with I Corinthians 14:3, if it does not edify, exhort or comfort, but rather is a strong word of condemnation with nothing to commend it in terms of the Scriptures, then my own spirit witnesses against it.

> *But he that prophesieth speaketh unto men to edification, and exhortation, and comfort* (I Corinthians 14:3).

During the last fourteen years I have had to do this on only two occasions out of the hundreds of messages I have heard in public meetings.

In some situations church leaders permit only "professional prophets." I call them "professional" without intending to be derogatory, but in effect everybody looks to these persons to bring a word of prophecy in accordance with the gift of prophecy referred to in I Corinthians 12, but they do not look to any other person.

I feel that there is confusion here between the gift of prophecy and the ministry of a prophet. In God's grace, some churches have acknowledged *prophets*, but we must remember that the ministry of prophecy is for everyone and we should all be able to participate in this ministry:

> *For ye may all prophesy one by one, that all may learn, and all may be comforted* (I Corinthians 14:31).

It is so in order that we may learn and be comforted.

I remember speaking in a church on the gifts of the Spirit, then encouraging church members to move in this gift. The Holy Spirit indicated to me that there were ten persons in that place through whom He desired to move that day, so I asked that no person should speak who had ever previously brought a word of prophecy or a message in a tongue.

The first message which came forth was anointed, and I sensed in my spirit that the person had not spoken out previously. The second message was good, and again came from a first-timer. But when the third message was brought I knew immediately that the person had frequently brought a message in that church.

After the lady had finished I asked if she had previously prophesied and she said yes. I then pointed out that I had asked that no person should bring a message who had prophesied before.

The fourth message was again from a beginner, but the fifth person who spoke out was a "professional prophet."

Despite my repeated requests, it continued to happen. Some people feel tremendous pressure (inwardly or from their peers) to bring a word, even in disregard of God's direction to the leadership of the meeting. Those who had been accustomed to prophesying did not resist bringing a word of prophecy, even though they were told not to do so and to allow others to speak. At least seventeen persons brought a word before I reached the required ten which the Lord had given me and whom He wished to encourage for the first time.

I have said previously that I believe the Holy Spirit speaks through one person at a time in the directing of a meeting. That person may be preaching, prophesying, or leading in worship. Whatever is the case, he or she should be very sensitive to what god is saying at that particular moment. I well remember when the Lord began to encourage me to bring my wife Pat into the gift of prophecy. He spoke clearly to me one night that He had given Pat a word of prophecy. She then brought it forth somewhat hesitantly, but the Holy Spirit said there was more. I urged her to bring more, until the whole message was presented.

Even today the Holy Spirit will show me on occasions that not the whole word of prophecy has been brought, and I then encourage the person to bring a further word.

As we continued to hold our prayer meetings, the numbers became so great that it was necessary to bring people into the basement of the house as well as into the family room and the lounge. (The center of worship was in the lounge and we had intercom speakers in the other rooms.) Imagine my concern one night when the Holy Spirit let me know there was a message in tongues among those gathered in the basement.

I did not know who was in the basement, or even if they were believers. However, moving in faith, I asked for a message in tongues to be brought from the basement and, sure enough, it flowed forth beautifully through the intercom system. The Holy Spirit then indicated that the interpretation was in the family room, and as I called for it somebody from that room brought forth a beautiful word of interpretation.

The obvious way in which the Spirit was moving created a tremendous spirit of faith in the meeting, not only inspiring me as a leader, but everyone else present, so that the Spirit of God was then able to bless and touch people mightily throughout the meeting.

Sometimes when I am speaking the Holy Spirit indicates to me that He is healing somebody of a particular condition. I may be led to stop at that point and express what I believe the Lord is saying. People will probably stand up at that moment, healed, or at least knowing that the power of God is falling upon them. This further heightens the faith and expectancy in the meeting.

Paul said that he did not come with excellency of speech or wisdom, "declaring unto you the testimony of God." His speech and preaching were not with enticing words of men's wisdom but in demonstration of the Spirit and of power:

> And my speech and my preaching was not with enticing words of man's wisdom, but in demonstration of the Spirit and of power (I Corinthians 2:4).

The Holy Spirit is always willing to demonstrate His love and His power if we are open to Him.

When only a few people are spiritually stimulated to prophesy in a church, others become discouraged. That is why Paul said that we should all prophesy in the ministry of prophesy. I believe that if all members were motivated to prophesy, God would speak mightily throughout the congregation.

Therefore, if you are acting in a leadership role remember that the Holy Spirit is the one leading the meeting through you, and you do not need to strive or struggle. Just let Him operate throughout the meeting, speaking through various persons as He leads. You will then find a great anointing coming over the meeting. The spirit of faith will be revived, and healings and deliverances will take place before your very eyes.

SEVENTEEN

Learning in Groups

When I have taught my understanding of the matters raised in this book and in particular the operation of the gifts I often encourage my hearers to form themselves into small groups of five or six persons. I then begin with encouraging people to move in the area of prophecy. I first of all ask that each person in the group says something in turn. It should be something to glorify God such as "God Loves me" or "God is here" or similar words. I then encourage that each person in the group speak a .second time but on this occasion I tell them to envisage that they are speaking on behalf of God. I ask them to speak out things which they would believe to speak to the group "I am here with you my people" or "I love you my people".

By this simple exercise one begins to encourage people to move out in this gift of prophecy. As they begin to step out further in faith and allow thoughts, or visions, or impressions, or even the audible voice of the Holy Spirit to speak to them we find that very rapidly the anointing falls upon the group as

God pours out his gift of prophecy in that group. Very quickly young Christians can indeed gain confidence and move in this gift.

I next encourage several people in the group to speak out in their tongue. They should do this in order and wait for an interpretation. Here again we are moving in faith and are encouraging Christians to move out in God. By carrying out this simple exercise we rapidly find that the anointing of the Holy Spirit falls and as people gain confidence they will speak out in their tongue and an interpretation would quickly follow. If we encourage people in the group to believe for a thought, or an impression or the audible voice of God or a vision then God is able to speak through the person bringing the interpretation and a great blessing falls on the group.

From this point it is easy to move into the other gifts for example, the word of knowledge. Here again I encourage people to reach out and allow God to give them a thought, or an impression, or hear His audible voice or receive a vision concerning some other person in the group. I do not ask them to centre on a particular person but just allow the Holy Spirit to bring a thought or an impression and the needs that they may have. Extraordinary things begin to happen as people open up to God and they find immediate confirmation of some of these thoughts and impressions. Sometimes it is the audible voice of the Holy Spirit or a vision through which God speaks to a person in the group. We find faith beginning to rise rapidly as people do confirm that the words of knowledge are correct. Similarly it is easy to encourage others into the gift of discernment by allowing them to bring a thought or an impression or a vision, or allowing the Holy Spirit to speak audibly to them and to tell them of spirits or forces which may be attacking another person. As this is confirmed and the person is prayed for a release takes place.

I then encourage people to believe for the gift of healings to operate. In fact, some of the words of knowledge may be related to healing needs of a person in the group, so as that person comes forward and the others allow the anointing of God to fall and they pray in God's love then healing takes place.

A further reference of the fact that we have the fragrance of God upon us is also clear in Paul's second letter to the Corinthians as follows:

> "*For we are unto God a sweet savour of Christ, in them that are saved and them that perish.*" (2 *Corinthians* 2:15).

The fragrance of the Holy Spirit should be upon us as we walk in this world. The world always senses the presence of God around the true believer.

Thus we find that we have indeed received an anointing and in the same way that Aaron felt that physical anointing upon his body so we too can feel the presence of God upon our physical body. This is why John was able to say so emphatically that we have an unction from the Holy Spirit. We should expect that anointing to fall upon us as we are witnessing for Jesus Christ, or we are preaching, or praying for the sick, or carrying out any other activity on the part of the Lord. As we open ourselves to the Holy Spirit then He is able to express himself through us by this anointing and we can physically feel his presence upon us. It is true that we walk by faith and not by sight but as we walk in faith we should expect the feeling of the anointing.

EIGHTEEN

Final Practical Insights

1. We should not minister when we are tired. There are times, of course, when we cannot avoid this. I find that when we are tired we are under a greater attack and it is harder to hear the voice of the Lord.

2. Remain humble. Remember that Satan will try to convince you that you are better than the next person. He will attack you in pride; this is the very reason for his fall. Those to whom you are ministering will immediately discern in the spirit whether you are humble or not.

3. Always act in love. If you are moving in God's love the Holy Spirit can move through you, and the person to whom you are ministering will have confidence in your ministry. He will know you are not judging him and he will be able to receive what God is offering him through you.

4. Always be open to God's call upon your life. God often uses the weakest vessel in an anointed way to bring His message.

5. Remember that God wants the gifts to be ministered in the body of Christ in order to build us up, inspire us and extend His kingdom. Never be afraid to move in the gifts of the Holy Spirit, for this is one of the principal ways in which the Holy Spirit is able to show His presence in a congregation. Then when the unbelieving come into our midst they will be able to say, "Truly, this is of God!"